M000216846

The Complete Handlebar Guide to

Bicycling the TransAm

Virginia to Oregon/ Washington

Fourth Edition

Stephanie Ager Kirz

Published by White Dog Press, Ltd.

This Fourth Edition comes ten years after the first printing in 2003. Needless to say, unfortunately the recession took a big bite out of the many mom and pop establishments along the route. Thanks to Byron Severinghaus and Jeanette Alexander, we made over 950 edits to phone numbers, addresses, and other details, and we are certain you'll find more. ENJOY!

THANK YOU FOR BUYING THIS BOOK,
AND SAFE JOURNEYS!

Dedicated to Howard L. Kirz, who dreamed the trip of a lifetime and let me pedal alongside.

Published by
White Dog Press, Ltd.
Pima Press, Imprint
321 High School Road Ste. D3, PMB 393
Bainbridge Island, WA 98110
E-mail:Whitedogpress@aol.com
www.whitedogpress.net

Second Edition, 2005
Third Edition, 2009
Fourth Edition, 2014

All photographs by Howard L. Kirz unless otherwise specified. Design by Stephanie Ager Kirz with additional design and publication consultations by Ghost River Images (ghostriverimages.com) and Jeanette Alexander Graphic Design (jalexgd@sounddsl.com).

A special thank you to the staff of *Adventure Cycling* for being such a big help with this book.

Cover and state heading-page photographs: Lolo Pass in Idaho, Greg Siple, Adventure Cycling

Library of Congress Control Number: 200309468

CONTENTS

MONTANA   Pages 146-158

IDAHO   Pages 161-170

OREGON   Pages 174-192

ALTERNATE: Pages 193-226

A NORTHERN ROUTE TO SEATTLE, WASHINGTON

INTRODUCTION

I. WHY I WROTE THIS BOOK

"This is the book we wish we'd had!"
When the original cyclists made their historic trek across America in 1976, they were young, didn't wear helmets, slept on the ground and prepared much of their own food. Indeed, even if you like to camp, every once in awhile it's nice to know where you can find a soft bed and good meal along the route. But no all-in-one resource was available. So I wrote this book for fellow cyclists it's the book we wish we'd had on out trip.

Finding well-placed campgrounds, accommodations and good food along a route that is rich in small-town history but lacking in recommendations was a challenge. We discovered that small towns with populations of less than 50 do not get put into many guidebooks. In fact, there are only a few towns on the TransAm route with populations of over 50,000. So finding a place to sleep BEFORE we biked 50 or 60 miles to the next town was an all-important research task.

Everyday I stuffed my saddle bags full of brochures and business cards from each small and smaller town that we rode through. At the end of each week, or when the waterproof zip-lock bag was bulging with pieces of paper, I mailed the package home to enable me to compile this guidebook.

Realistic Daily Itineraries - Perfect for Short or Long Trips
You don't have to ride 4,000 miles to use and enjoy this book. This trip was my husband's dream. It might have been my nightmare, but thanks to his careful planning no day was beyond my limits. I had never ever dreamed of doing such a thing. It wasn't even on my Top 100 list. However, with advance training and a realistic day-by-day route that left us plenty of time for exploring the town or countryside every afternoon, the trip was a supreme adventure. The key to our success was in leaving early in the morning and getting the miles done before lunch; that way we got to the next town with lots of left-over energy.

II. TRAINING

Yuk, Training!

Unless you're 18, training is one key to how well you'll do on this trip. And I hate training. However, with the help of an Excel spread sheet and tremendous incentives (you can eat anything you want and not gain weight), the training was tolerable.

The trip is approximately 4,000 miles and 148,000 feet of elevation gain. That's equivalent to climbing Mount Rainier 10 times on a bike. So, hill-climbing and endurance are all important. In addition, you're carrying all your belongings; so you need to get ready to carry that load. Plan on increasing your training mileage by 10 percent per week initially and 5 to 7.5 percent the last month. Start adding the weight and practicing with your panniers or BOB by at least the final month. There are several on-line coaches and many good references on the subject. I've included a copy of my own training schedule as a reference point. As you can see, travel, weather and health all conspired to keep me from reaching my targets every week. But that's life, and by the time we departed I was definitely trained and ready.

Example: Stephanie's Actual Training Chart

Week	Sun	Mon	Tues	Wed	Thurs	Fri	Sat	Target	Actual	Accum
1-Jan	travel	travel	travel	15	8	rest	rest	85	88*	88
8-Jan	65*	18	rest	30	15	15	22	100	100	188
15-Jan	30	rest	rest	45	20	32	31	110	113	301
22-Jan	63	rest	rest	46	rest	14	travel	121	122	423
29-Jan	travel	rest	rest	31	18	26	43	133	133	556
5-Feb	rest	rest	29	31	rest	36	flu	146	96	652
12-Feb	flu	flu	flu	19	21	78	rest	146	118	770
19-Feb	61	rest	29	50	rest	31	rest	161	171	941
26-Feb	78	rest	22	50	24	rest	62	177	174	1115
5-Mar	travel	travel	12	15	23	45	rest	190	157	1272
12-Mar	63	21	66	22	rest	46	travel	204	218	1490
19-Mar	10	travel	travel	32	80	52	21	220	195	1685
26-Mar	53	rest	30	59	rest	rest	63	236	205	1890
2-Apr	56	rest	64	60	rest	rest	70	254	250	2140
9-Apr	travel	travel	travel	travel	7	30	61	273	98	2238
16-Apr	71	rest	27	50	30	rest	rest	293	178	2416
23-Apr	70	rest	rest	20	rest	34	51	300	175	2591
1-May	GO!									

Notes:
1) * Some of this mileage is added to week before or after.
2) Target mileage Jan-Feb is previous week's target + 10%, then + 7.5%.

III. NUTRITION - HOW MANY MILES CAN YOU GO ON A THREE MUSKETEERS?

"Burn, Baby, Burn"

One thing we learned quickly while training: You can't run an engine without fuel. You need calories to fuel muscles, but just how many calories does a bike-mile burn? Hence the term "burn rate." The big problem in everyday life is eating too many calories, but for me, at 105 pounds, it was more of a challenge to eat enough calories to keep both me and the bike going without bonking.

We learned to calculate the needed calories with material we discovered on the web and in Dr. Richard Raforth's excellent book, *High-Performance Bicycling Nutrition*. We figured out that you burn about 350 calories in approximately 15 miles on a flat surface. For example, on a relatively flat ride, if you ride 75 miles, you need to eat 1,750 calories before, during and after the ride to maintain body weight and fuel efficiency. In fact, on long rides it'generally better to eat something every hour or every 15 miles.

Climbing hills obviously burns more calories, and big people on hills burn more calories than smaller people on hills. Little people like me had to eat 4,000 calories on a 75-mile hilly ride, for example. But the constant search for calories wasn't the only challenge. You need the right calories with a high percentage of complex and simple carbohydrates. Dr. Atkins dieters, eat your hearts out.

Some Nutritional Rules to Remember
1. Carbos, Quick

Carbo-loading the night before a long-distance ride works well. Also, studies show that you need to replenish the carbos no later than two hours after a ride; 30 minutes is best for better absorption.

2. Meat is Neat

Whether you eat meat or not, you need some protein during the day. This helps with muscle repair. That's why you eat some cheese, slather a bagel with peanut butter or have some protein like eggs in the morning. Personally, I always thought pancakes were protein until I started reading the references.

3. Eat Before You're Hungry

We were never hungry because we just got into the habit of eating small snacks throughout the day to keep refueling. If your stomach starts aching, you've waited too long. Make sure that you always carry extra food. Don't wait for that grocery-store stop 20 miles down the road. Unfortunately, it may not be there. Those Mom and Pop grocery stores along the route come and go.

4. Drink Before You're Thirsty

Hydrate, hydrate, hydrate. Lack of water will take you out of the ride faster than lack of food. One day in Missouri, when the temperature was 95 and the humidity was 95, we went through 462 ounces of liquid in 52 miles. Remember to mix it with a sports-drink powder for electrolytes. Plain water won't do it. Also, ice-cold water will absorb much faster than tepid water if you get dehydrated.

A Few Personal Discoveries

1. Frequent small snacks digest more easily. Big meals don't get a chance to get digested, and they just sit there in your stomach and churn. Yuk. That's why we tried to get the biking for each day done before lunch.

2. Bagels, bananas, pasta, pancakes, boiled red potatoes, health food bars, fig newtons, apple newtons, anykindofnewtons, cheese pizza, pretzels and Cheetos (I know they're not food but I love them!) all worked well for us.

3. Small pieces of candy can help, like little Snickers.

4. Coffee helps. But, then, we're from the coffee capital of North America, Seattle, so what do we know?

5. No matter how many times I tried to eat french fries or anything fried while riding, it wouldn't sit well.

IV. EQUIPMENT

Howard, my husband, did all the research and planning in this
department and, thanks to him, we never had sore bottoms (I tried four
different bike seats before leaving home) or a flat tire in 4,000 miles.
Most important is having a bike that fits properly and will stand up
to the road wear and weight of the bags. Breakdowns are a problem,
especially when you're out in the middle of nowhere. We had a deal with
our local bike shop on Bainbridge Island – B.I.Cycle Shop – to FedEx
or Priority Mail us parts if we got stuck somewhere. But we were lucky
and we had a well-equipped tool kit for minor adjustments. In addition,
we took a bike-repair class in advance of the trip, just in case.

Our Actual Bike Equipment
• Two Independent Fabrications "Independence" model steel touring
frames. We find that steel rides more comfortably for us than other
metals. Day after day, we got on these bikes and cruised along as though
riding in an old Caddy with the top down.

• 32 x 700C Rhino-Lite tandem-style rims with Conti Top Touring tires
and 36 double-tapered stainless spokes.

• 24, 34, 44 Shimano XT cranksets. You need to get up and down all
those hills.

• 11-32, 8-speed rear sprockets.

• Avid Shorty cantilever brake sets. Heavily-loaded bikes require heavy-
duty stopping power.

• Three water bottles each (Camelbacks are uncomfortable for us on
long trips).

• BOB Trailer (for Howard).

• Bruce Gordon front and rear Pannier racks (for me).

• Front and rear Panniers with waterproof liners.

• Handlebar bag with map case (for Howard).

• Rear Rack bag – Six Pack (for me).

• Rear-view mirror attached to glasses, helmet, or bike.

• An assortment of headlights, flashing tail lights, fenders, bike horns, cyclometers.

• A three-month supply of Sabre (big time pepper spray) in a top tube, bike-mounted holster).

V. SAMPLE MEN'S PACKING LIST (Howard's)

Bike Clothes & Gear

Bike Shorts (3)
Black Bike Tights (1)
Bike Tops (3)
Bike Gloves (1)
Glove Liners
Black Polypro Turtlenecks (2)
Black Polarfleece Pullover (1)
Head Caps (2)
Headband-earflaps (1)
Bike Glasses with Case and Blades
Bike Vest
Lightweight Wind Jacket
Bike Rain Jacket (could be combined with above)
Bike Socks (3-4)
Wool Bike Socks (1)
Bike Shoes
Bike Shoe Covers
Heart Rate Monitor
Chamois Butter

Street Clothes

Cotton Shorts (1)
Swimsuit (1)
Short Sleeve Shirts (2)
T-Shirts (4)
Cotton T-Neck (1)
Sweater/Sweatshirt (1)
Underwear (5)
Extra Glasses/Clips-ons (1)
Handkerchiefs (2)
Jeans or Khaki Pants (1-2)
Walking Sandals (1)
Loafers
White Socks (4)
Belt (1)
Credit Card/Money Belt

Toiletries

Shaving Cream
Aftershave
Sun Screen
Chapstick
Toothbrush/Toothpaste/
    Dental Floss
Lomotil/Bactrim/Tylenol
    /Benadryl
Tums
Hydrocortisone/Neosporin
Band-Aids
Insect Repellent
Vitamins
Razors (3)
Deodorant
Nail Clippers, Scissors
Comb
Toilet Paper
Cigar Cutter!

Other

Camera/Film
Spiral Notebook/Pen
ATT Cell Phone
Bike Triangle
Flashlight
Travel Alarm Clock
Address Book with e-mail addresses
Credit Card/Driver's License
Data Sheet: (Customer ID/passwords, web ID #s/passwords,
    financial account #s/passwords
Keys: House/Bike Locks

Bike Tools

4-6 Spare Tubes
Bike Tool Set: Spoke wrench, chain tool, hex wrenches, small crescent,
    screwdrivers, patch kits, tire boots
Bike Lube/Cleaning: Teflon oil, orange cleaner, WD 40
Bike Rags: Red versus disposable
Tire Pumps/Pressure Gauge
Spare Spokes
Extra Rear Skewer for BOB
Adventure Cycling Maps - TransAmerica Trail, Sections 1-12
Insect Repellent
Folding Knife
Gatorade/Containers
Spare Cables
Lock/Chain

And most importantly (but not available until I wrote it!)
The Complete Handlebar Guide to Bicycling the TransAm

VI. OTHER

1976 Bike Centennial – The Origin of the TransAmerica Trail
The TransAmerica Trail was the route that made cross-country cycling famous. It all started with an idea by Greg Siple, co-founder of Bikecentennial, to tour America on a bike in honor of the country's Bicentennial in 1976. Greg, his wife June, Dan and Lys Burden and an inspired group of enthusiasts began forming that first ride and mapping the inaugural 4,250-plus-mile route from Williamsburg, Virginia, to Oregon in 1973. That first ride, called the Bikecentennial, left Williamsburg in June 1976, and eventually attracted over 4,000 riders from all over the globe. Thus were the very roots that formed Bikecentennial renamed Adventure Cycling Association, based in Missoula, Montana. It is these maps of the TransAmerica route that we have referenced in our book, and it is with great appreciation that they, not us, do meticulous mapping for this and their other popular routes across the country.

Adventure Cycling Association
PO Box 8308
Missoula, MT 59807
800-721-8719
www.adventurecycling.org

1976 Bikecentennial Finishers
Photo courtesy Adventure Cycling Assoc.

Kirz Cross-Country Caper – Keeping an on-line web journal

We kept a web journal of our trip, thanks to Neil Gunton, who hosts a web site for bicyclists to post their trips on. With the help of the local libraries in small towns across America, we used their computers for our internet access. Andrew Carnegie supplied the funds to build over 5,000 libraries around the world in the early 1900s, and many of them are in these small towns. People ask us, "Did we carry a digital camera?" No, we simply used a point-and-shoot and mailed the negatives to Film Stop in Seattle, who then posted them on their web site. We were able to transfer these photos to our web journal as we traveled across the country. Neil perfected the web site, and now you can view the photos separately without the text just like a slide show. Friends, relatives and complete strangers were able to keep us company on our trip by signing the guestbook, which gave us great comfort on this long journey.

Check out our original narrative journal at:
Kirz.crazyguyonabike.com

Neil Gunton, webmaster, has posted over 100 cycling journals on his free web site and continually upgrades his site to make it user-friendly. Be sure to check out www.crazyguyonabike.com before your trip.

VII. ABOUT THIS BOOK

Mileage and Elevation Estimates

The mileage for 10 states is coordinated with Adventure Cycling maps. In Washington State as of this writing, there are no maps for the mid-state route we followed. Accordingly the mileage for Washington State is an approximation based on our own cyclometer readings. Mileage and elevations are our best estimates and should not be viewed as precise.

Bicycle With Caution

Bicycling across the US has risks and rewards. Among the risks you will doubtless experience: severe weather, heavy traffic, highway construction. Some of the routes recommended in this book and by Adventure Cycling do not have good shoulders. My best advice is to bike carefully and defensively every day throughout your trip.

Route Updates

Things change, and so do the routes over time due to increased traffic and growth. New, improved routes and information can be found on Adventure Cycling's web page: www.adventurecycling.org.

Your Feedback, Please

Your feedback is important. Unfortunately some of those Mom and Pop motels, eateries and even bike shops go out-of-business. Please let us know when you see a change and we'll gladly incorporate it into this book. E-mail me at: whitedogpress@aol.com or write us at White Dog Press, 321 High School Road, Ste. D3, PMB 393, Bainbridge Island, WA 98110. Please note that many prices for accommodations have increased. Thank you.

Have a wonderful, safe journey!
Stephanie Ager Kirz, Publisher

Note: For more bicycling adventure stories (Sicily, Ireland, Scotland, Thailand, Paris) go to **www.whitedogpress.net**

LEGEND*

$ 75 or less
$$ 75-95
$$$ 95-130
$$$$ 130 plus

✖ = Restaurant
▽ = Breakfast
🏖 = Pool
▣ = Coin Laundry

 I ride, therefore I TransAm.®

JAMESTOWN
THE FIRST PERMANENT
COLONY OF THE
ENGLISH PEOPLE
THE BIRTHPLACE OF
VIRGINIA
AND OF
THE UNITED STATES
· MAY 13 · 1607 ·

VIRGINIA
12 Days - 576.5 Miles

Birthplace of eight Presidents, Virginia is a biker's paradise. Full of avid cyclists, the state has an active program through the Department of Transportation with a guide and maps for additional routes. Your trip begins in historic Williamsburg and ends in Breaks Interstate Park on the border of Kentucky. In between lie hundreds of years of American Revolution and Civil War history. Some bikers say that the terrain is hilly. It's far less hilly than Kentucky and makes for a good warm-up for what lies ahead.

VIRGINIA FACTS & RESOURCES

Department of Tourism
901 E Byrd Street
Richmond, VA 23219
800-847-4882
800-VISITVA
www.virginia.org

Virginia State Chamber of Commerce
919 E Main St,
Suite 900
Richmond, VA 23219
800-644-1607
www.vachamber.com

Virginia Bicycling Guide
Department of Transportation
800-835-1203
vabiking@vdot.state.va.us.

Virginia Campground Information
800-9CAMPVA
www.virginiacampgrounds.org

Fast Facts
Population: 6 million plus
Capital: Richmond
Flower: American Dogwood
Bird: Cardinal

Key Dates in History
1607   Jamestown settled
1775   Revolutionary War begins
1776   Declaration of Independence signed
1789   George Washington becomes first president
1861   Civil War begins
1865   Civil War ends

There are two ways to begin this trip-of-a-lifetime. Either stay in Yorktown and head immediately westward from the Yorktown Victory Monument, the official starting point of the TransAm, or stay in Williamsburg and use Day 0 for a "shake-out" roundtrip ride to Yorktown. By following the latter strategy, which is recommended, you'll have enough time to really enjoy this historic area.

If you're staying in Williamsburg, check with your hotel or campground staff for the closest entrance to the "Colonial Parkway," built by the Civilian Conservation Corps in the 1930s. It's the road to Yorktown but it's sometimes tough to find.

As is the custom of TransAm riders, be sure to dip your wheels in the Atlantic, actually the Yorktown River, at the Yorktown Public Beach before heading back to Williamsburg.

PLACES TO STAY

WILLIAMSBURG

Quality Inn Historic Area
600 Bypass Road
Williamsburg, VA 23185
800-228-5151, 757-220-2800
$$$ ⛵🏊▣

La Quinta Inn & Suites
814 Capital Landing Road
Williamsburg, VA 23185
800-753-3757, 757-229-0200
$$$ ✕🏊▣

Hampton Inn & Suites Historic District
911 Capital Landing Road
Williamsburg, VA 23185
888-370-0981, 757-941-1777
$$$ ⛵🏊

Quality Inn Historic East – Busch Gardens Area
505 York Street
Williamsburg, VA 23185
800-228-5151, 757-220-3100
$$$ ⛵🏊▣

CAMPING

Anvil Campground
5243 Moretown Road
Williamsburg, VA 23188
757-565-2300
3 miles from Colonial
Williamsburg.

Williamsburg Resort KOA
4000 Newman Road
Williamsburg, VA 23188
800-KOA-1733, 757-565-2907
www.williamsburgkoa.com
6 miles from Colonial
Williamsburg.

FOOD & DINING

Unlimited options.

PLACES TO STAY

YORKTOWN (population 300)

Yorktown Motor Lodge
8829 George Washington
Memorial Highway, Rt. 17
Yorktown, VA 23692
800-950-4003, 757-898-5451
$$-$$$ 🏊
3 miles from Yorktown.

Duke of York Hotel
508 Water Street
Yorktown, VA 23690
757-898-3232
$$ 🍴🏊

Marl Inn B&B
220 Church Street
Yorktown, VA 23690
757-898-3859
$$$ ☕
Discount to cyclists. Will allow
some camping on lawn if reserved
in advance with owner.

Grace Episcopal Church
111 Church Street/PO Box 123
Yorktown, VA 23690
757-898-3261
E-mail: ebakkum@cox.net
Elsa Bakkum has organized a
hospitality group to host cyclists.

CAMPING

Newport News Campground
13564 Jefferson Avenue
Newport News, VA 23063
800-203-8322, 757-888-3333
www.nnparks.com/parks_nn.php
5 miles to Yorktown on unofficial
bike trail. Check for directions.

FOOD AND DINING

Waterstreet Landing
524 Water Street
Yorktown, VA 23692
757-886-5890
Pizza, sandwiches, homemade
desserts.

A ceremonial dip in the Atlantic

Yorktown Pub
540 Water Street
Yorktown, VA 23692
757-886-9964
Soft-shelled crab sandwiches,
gumbo, cash only.

Beach Delly
524 Water Street
Yorktown, VA 23690
757-886-5890

James River Pie Company
1804 Jamestown Rd
Williamsburg, VA 23185
757-229-775
www.buyapie.com

SPECIAL INTEREST

Colonial Williamsburg
800-HISTORY, 757-253-2277
www.colonialwilliamsburg.org
This 230-acre outdoor museum
features 88 original structures
and hundreds of reconstructed
buildings representing life during
the 1770s in Williamsburg, the
former capitol of Virginia. A cast
of hundreds dressed in the clothing
of the era enact daily activities.
Admission Charge: $33.00.

Yorktown Battlefield
Colonial National Historical Park
& Museum / Visitor Center
1000 Colonial Parkway
Yorktown, VA 23690
757-898-3400
www.nps.gov/colo
"The battlefield in particular
surpasses all others in the care

with which the remains are
preserved and explained to
the visitor and Yorktown is an
excellent example." Fields of
Battle, John Keegan.

Victory Monument
Main Street
Yorktown, VA 23690
Last victorious battle of the
American Revolution in 1781.
Official start of the 1976
Bikecentennial Bike Route.

RESOURCES

**Williamsburg Convention
& Visitors Bureau**
800-368-6511
www.VisitWilliamsburg.com

**Williamsburg Hotel & Motel
Association** 800-899-9462

Bike's Unlimited
141 Monticello Avenue
Williamsburg, VA 23185
757-229-4620
www.bikewilliamsburg.com

Celebrate Yorktown Committee
757-890-3300, 757-890-3500
www.yorkcounty.gov/cyc

**Williamsburg Chamber of
Commerce**
757-229-6511, 800-368-6511

You won't be riding far in bike miles today but you'll be traveling through nearly 200 years of our country's history. Once again, find the closest entrance to the Colonial Parkway, but this time head west along the peaceful James River towards Jamestown.

Sites along the way include the Colonial National Historic Park-Original Jamestown Site, first English settlement on the continent.

From Jamestown there is a new bike path to the Chickahominy River bridge.

At 15.5 miles, watch out for the steel deck on the Chickahominy River bridge; it can be quite slippery so you might consider walking your bike in moist weather. You'll pass Sherwood Forest, the first of a series of grand 18th and 19th century plantations and the only one occupied by two American presidents, William Henry Harrison in the 18th century and John Tyler in the 19th.

Charles City itself isn't a city at all but you'll find Haupt's Country Store owned by the same family for more than 100 years.

PLACES TO STAY

North Bend Plantation
12200 Weyanoke Road
Charles City, VA 23030
804-829-5176
www.northbendplantation.com
$$$$ 🏊
Meals are available if requested in advance.
Run by descendants of the original owners, this B&B is located on a 500-acre working plantation once inhabited by General Sheridan. Call owner for directions. 1-2 miles off the main highway and about 2 miles from the only grocery store.

James River Plantation B&B
4800 John Tyler Memorial Hwy
Charles City, VA 23030
804-829-2962
www.edgewoodplantation.com
$$$$ ☕🏊
Meal plan available/recommended.

CAMPING

Willis United Methodist Church Hostel
19 miles from Charles City on SR 156 at Willis.
804-795-5630

FOOD & DINING

Haupt's Country Store
11911 John Tyler Memorial Hwy
Charles City, VA 23030
804-829-2418
Family operated since 1893, it's the only grocery in the Charles City area.

Food In Route: The only food stops between Williamsburg and Charles City are in the surrounding area of Jamestown with a cafe in the Jamestown Settlement and a few other spots.

James River Pie Company
Route 31 outside of Jamestown.
Great gourmet pizza by the slice, pecan pie, picnic tables.

7-11
Route 31 outside of Jamestown.
Across street from Pie Company.

SPECIAL INTEREST

Colonial National Historic Park – The Original Jamestown Site
1368 Colonial Parkway
Jamestown, VA 23081
757-229-9776

Historic Museum Settlement
757-253-4883
historicjamestowne.org
22.5-acre historic site of the first permanent English settlement and the birthplace of Virginia and the United States, May 13, 1607. New archeological dig in progress.

James River Plantations
Charles City, VA 23030
804-829-5004
www.jamesriverplantations.org
Open to the Public.

Berkeley Plantation
Charles City, VA 23030
804-829-6018
www.berkeleyplantation.com
6 miles west of Charles City.
Site of first official Thanksgiving in 1619.

Sherwood Forest Plantation
14501 John Tyler Memorial Hwy
Charles City, VA 23030
804-829-5377
www.sherwoodforest.org
Once owned by 10th US President John Tyler, it is the longest frame house in America.

Shirley Plantation
501 Shirley Plantation Rd
Charles City, VA 23030
800-232-1613
www.shirleyplantation.com
Home of famous Hill-Carter
family for 11 generations.

Jamestown Settlement
Commonwealth of Virginia
2110 Jamestown Rd
Williamsburg, VA 23185
www.historyisfun.org
757-253-4838

Heading west from Charles River in the morning, you'll pass more historic James River plantations, including Evelynton, Berkeley and Shirley before turning north and entering Civil War country.

Eighty percent of the Civil War was fought in the state of Virginia, much of it in the area surrounding Richmond. As you head in that direction, you'll pass numerous battlefields, some marked by cannons and others by graves. The "Seven Days Battle," McClelland's failed 1862 campaign against Lee, comprises the Malvern Hill, Gaines Mill and White Oak Swamp sites. Farther on at 35 miles, the Richmond Battlefield Park Visitors Center, Cold Water Unit is a particularly nice place to soak up some history as well as a lunchtime picnic and nap. The combined casualty rate here numbered 16,000 Union and Confederate soldiers; so stay alert for ghosts.

You'll crisscross Interstate 295 a few times and dodge some suburban traffic near Mechanicsville as you pass north of Richmond. Eventually you'll end up in the more peaceful suburb of Ashland for the night.

PLACES TO STAY

Hampton Inn
705 England Street
Ashland, VA 23005
1-800-HAMPTON
804-752-8444
$$$ ⛶ ✗ ▣

Henry Clay Inn
114 N Railroad Avenue
Ashland, VA 23005
804-798-3100
henryclayinn.com
$$$$ ⛶ ✗

Super 8 Motel
806-B England Street
Ashland, VA 23005
804-752-7000, 800-536-0719
$$ ⛶ ≋

CAMPING

Americamps Richmond North
11322 Air Park Road
Ashland, VA 23005
800-628-2802, 804-798-5298
www.americacamps.com
4 miles SE of Ashland.

FOOD & DINING

All restaurants are located in
downtown Ashland.

Ashland Coffee & Tea House
Retro '60s hang-out with local beer.
www.ashlandcoffeeandtea.com

The Ironhorse Restaurant
Steak and bar.
www.ironhorserestaurant.com

Cracker Barrel
Country cooking.
www.crackerbarrel.com
McDonalds, Pizza Hut and other
fast food chains.

SPECIAL INTEREST

**Richmond National Battlefield
Park**
Civil War Visitor Center
National Park Service
3215 E. Broad Street
Richmond, VA 23223
888-CIVIL WAR, 804-226-1981
www.nps.gov/rich/

**Ashland Historic Self-Guided
Walking Tour**
800-897-1479
Map available at Visitor Center.

Randolph-Macon College
204 Henry St
Ashland VA 23005
800-888-1762, 804-752-7200
Founded in 1830, it is the oldest
Methodist college in the US.

RESOURCES

Cycles Ed
12275 Maple Street
Ashland, VA 23005
804-798-7046

**Ashland/Hanover Visitor Center
– 1923 Train Station**
112 N Railroad Avenue
Ashland, VA 23005
800-897-1479, 804-752-6766
www.town.ashland.va.us

Cobblestone Bicycles
102 South Railroad Ave.
Ashland, VA 23005
804-752-4851

Hills begin to make their appearance today as you leave the Ashland Coffee House, a good place to get that morning cup of Java, and ride towards the Blue Ridge Parkway. You'll pass rolling pastures of Virginia horse farms and stables a la Robert Duvall and other country gentlemen. You'll also pass near Patrick Henry's ("Give me liberty or give me death") birthplace in Scotchtown. Louisa County is a dry county so don't get your heart set on an after-ride beer stop. Louisa County is also a tough place to find accommodations. Mineral is a better bet than Louisa if you can get reservations at the big splurge Littlepage Inn. This is Mineral's only place to stay, but they are frequently booked for weddings. Otherwise, you'll end up bicycling 6.5 miles down the road to Louisa.

PLACES TO STAY

MINERAL

Littlepage Inn B&B
9 miles N. on US 522
15701 Monrovia Rd
Mineral, VA 23117
800-248-1803, 540-854-9861
www.littlepage.com
$$$$ ☕, Meals on request.
1811 plantation home set on 150 acres. National Register of Homes.

FOOD & DINING

Joe's Place/Mineral Restaurant
42 Davis Hwy
Mineral, VA 23117
540-894-4927
Mineral's favorite spot.

PLACES TO STAY

LOUISA
Whistle Stop B&B
318 Main Street
Louisa, VA 23093
540-967-2911
$$ ☕
Call first. Previously for sale.

Rebel Motel
112 Jefferson Hwy
Louisa, VA 23093
540-967-1585
$

**High Point Marina and
Lighthouse Inn**
4634 Courthouse Road
Mineral, VA 23117
540-895-5249
$$
Units, fishing and barbecue on the
lake. 7 miles north of Mineral.

CAMPING

Christopher Run Campground
6478 Zachery Taylor Hwy
Mineral, VA 23117
540-894-4744
www.christopherruncampground.com

Mineral Volunteer Fire Dept.
Call ahead: 540-894-5660

FOOD & DINING

Fast Food Chains in Louisa:
Pizza Hut – Serves beer.

Hardees

McDonald's

SPECIAL INTEREST

**Home of Patrick Henry –
National Historic Landmark**
Off Route 54, on West Patrick
Henry Hwy.
Rt. 671, Scotchtown Road
Scotchtown, VA
804-227-3500
E-mail: scotchtownAPVA@aol.com

Approximately 9 miles west
of Ashland. Built in 1719, it
is among the oldest surviving
plantation houses in Virginia.
This was Patrick Henry's home
during his most active years and
during the American Revolution.
Open for guided tours.

Mount Anna Visitor Center
Mineral, VA 23117

Patrick Henry's Scotchtown
16120 Chiswell Ln
Beaverdam, VA 23015
804-227-3500
preservationvirginia.org/visit/
historic-properties/patrick-henrys-
scotchtown

RESOURCES

**Louisa County Visitor
Information**
540-967-0944, 540-854-9119
www.visitlouisa.com

Mineral Volunteer Fire Dept.
201 1st St, Mineral, VA 23117
540-894-5660

Note: If you stayed in Louisa, you'll take US 33 eastward to intersect with CR 605, the main AC route headed west out of Mineral.
Beautiful paved roads await you today as you pass several wineries and numerous horse ranches with signs touting "Virginia-bred mares." The hills continue to roll and the grades slowly steepen. Make sure you leave time to tour Jefferson's Monticello (49.5 miles) before heading into Charlottesville. Jefferson commissioned the Lewis and Clark Expedition from this site, and many artifacts of the trip remain in the mansion. Both Presidents Jefferson and Madison were born in this countryside. Charlottesville is home to the lovely University of Virginia and a great place to catch up on email or run errands.

PLACES TO STAY

Budget Inn
140 Emmet Street N
Charlottesville, VA 22901
800-273-5144. 434-293-5141
$$

Hampton Inn & Suites
900 W Main Street
Charlottesville, VA 22903
www.hampsuites.com
888-370-0981
$$$ ⬠☕🏊▣

Marriott Courtyard
1201 W Main Street
Charlottesville, VA 22903
800-321-2211, 434-977-1700
www.marriot.com
$$$ ✕🏊

Super 8 Motel
390 Greenbriar Drive
Charlottesville, VA 22901
800-536-0719
www.super8.com
$$ ☕

CAMPING

Charlottesville KOA
(Formerly Cambrae Lodge KOA)
3825 Red Hill Road
Charlottesville, VA 22903
800-562-1743, 434-296-9881
See directions on AC map #12.
10 miles south of Monticello.
Off-route 9.4 miles.

Palmyra Camp Friendship
1.5 miles past Palmyra on US 15
573 Friendship Rd
Palmyra, 22963
434-589-8950

FOOD AND DINING

Food In Route:
Take along extra food and water.
From Mineral the first food stop
used to be 18.5 miles at Kent's
Store, now closed. Next store is
a little past Palmyre. There are no
sandwiches but you can purchase
a fishing license at **The Wheaton's
Rivanna Grocery**. **Tinsley's
Restaurant** is right around the
corner for sandwiches.
Intersection of 15 S & 53 W.

On "The Corner"
University Student hang-out.

Littlejohn's NY Deli
1427 University Ave
Charlottesville, VA 22903
434-977-0588
Open 24/7. Numerous delis, bagel
and coffee shops near campus.

SPECIAL INTEREST

**Jefferson's Vineyards Tours &
Tasting**
1353 Thomas Jefferson Parkway
Charlottesville, VA 22902
800-272-3042, 434-977-3042
www.jeffersonvineyards.com
Open daily 11-5.

Thomas Jefferson's Monticello
431 Thomas Jeffferson Prkwy
Charlottesville, WA 22902
434-984-9800
www.monticello.org
2 miles SE of Charlottesville near
intersection of Route 20 S and
I-64. Daily guided Historic Home
and Garden Tours. Lewis & Clark
Expedition was conceived here.

**Historic Downtown
Charlottesville**
Free trolley.

University of Virginia
Computer Center at Cocke Hall.
434-924-0311

RESOURCES

Blue Ridge Mountain Sports
1125 N Emmet Street
Charlottesville, VA 22903
434-977-4400
www.brms.com

Blue Wheel Bicycles
941 2nd St SE
Charlottesville, VA 22902
434-977-1870

Extreme Sports
629 Berkmar
Charlottesville, VA 22903
434-975-1900
www.cvillebike.com

Performance Bike Shop
234 Zan Road
Charlottesville, VA 22903
434-963-9161
www.performancebike.com

**Good source of information
about Charlottesville:**
www.virginia.edu/exploring.html

Thomas Jefferson's Monticello with spring blooms. Photo: CJMckendry, IstockPhoto.

DAY 5 CHARLOTTESVILLE TO ROCKFISH GAP (AFTON) or WAYNESBORO, VA
Mileage: 29 or 32
Est. Elevation: 3,500
AC Map:12:144, 143

This short but hilly day ends at the Blue Ridge Parkway. Along the way you'll make a visit to the famous Cookie Lady (or site of the Cookie Lady) several miles from the top, 27 miles from Charlottesville. The first 10 miles take you through rolling farmlands, horse farms, one-lane bridges, wild roses, clematis and big mansions. Horse farms turn into orchards with fruit stands of apples and peaches in season. A suburban paradise, Beemers and Volvo station wagons abound. The rest of the day gets a bit hillier. June Curry, the Cookie Lady, is a legend with TransAm cyclists; and, if you're lucky, you'll get a tour of her Bike House, jam-packed with memorabilia from cyclists all over the world.

One man owns the whole mountaintop of Rockfish Gap; so there's only one motel. In the Gap you can get heavy fog.

PLACES TO STAY

AFTON
The Inn at Afton
185 Afton Circle
Afton, VA 22980
800-860-8559, 540-942-5201
$$ 🏊 🍴
Junction of Skyline Drive and Blue Ridge Parkway (1-64 & 250)

Afton Mountain B&B
10273 Rockfish Valley Hwy
Afton, VA 22920
800-769-6844, 540-456-6844
www.aftonmountain.com
$$ ▱
Left on 151 off 250 as you approach Rockfish Gap. Call owners for exact directions.

FOOD AND DINING

Food In Route:
Wyant Grocery Store
434-823-1299
Whitehall
Est. in 1914 and known for their steamed hotdogs. Good for breakfast. 12 miles from Charlottesville.

The Inn at Afton
Breakfast and dinner only, and in the lounge on weekends.

Chevron Gas Station & C Store
Located at junction below Inn at Afton. Limited supplies.

WAYNESBORO
Pop: 18,500

Waynesboro is 3 miles downhill from the top of the gap in the Shenandoah Valley. But remember, if you have to go down, you'll need to go back up to the Gap to resume the route.

Comfort Inn
15 Windy Grove Ln
Waynesboro, VA 22980
866-365-9867, 540-932-3060
$$ 🏊
5 miles from the gap, easy to find.

Belle Hearth B&B
320 S Wayne Ave.
Waynesboro, VA 22980
800-949-6993 - 540-943-1910
www.bellehearth.com
$$ ☕

The Colony House Motel
494 Three Notched Mountain Hwy 250 E
Waynesboro, VA 22980

540-942-4156
$$,☕🏊
One mile from Gap.

FOOD & DINING

Numerous fast food and restaurants in Waynesboro.

CAMPING

Waynesboro Campground
1125 Eastside Hwy
Waynesboro, VA 22980
540-943-9573
Pool, groceries. 5 miles outside of Waynesboro at intersection of 250 and 340 N.

SPECIAL INTEREST

Rockfish Gap Tourism Visitor's Center
130 Afton Circle
Afton, VA 22920
540-943-5187
www.virginia.org
Open 9-5 daily.

Waynesboro Public Library
600 S Wayne Ave
Waynesboro, VA 22980
540-942-6746
DSL computer lines.

Rockfish Gap Outfitters
1461 E Main Street
Waynesboro, VA 22980
540-943-1461
www.rockfishgapoutfitters.com

Waynesboro Heritage Museum
420 W Main St
Waynesboro, VA 22980
540-943-3943
Free admission.

Greater Augusta
Chamber of Commerce
30 Ladd Rd
Fishersville, VA 22939
540-324-1133

June Curry, the famous "Cookie Lady" at
Afton. She was there for the first TransAms
riders in 1976.

Many cyclists consider the Blue Ridge Parkway's nearly 500 miles some of America's best biking. You'll get a short sample of the Parkway's allure and scenic vistas today. The route is lined with pink rhododendrons and dogwood. Look for the Humpback Rocks Visitor Center 5.2 miles from the Gap. There's a steep 2- mile downhill into Vesuvius from Parkway. Lexington books up in the summer with the Virginia Horse Show and college graduations; so make sure that you've secured a place to stay or camp before you get into town. Once in Lexington, visit the Virginia Military Institute, VMI, where Professor Stonewall Jackson haunts the hallways along with the ghosts of Generals Robert E. Lee, George Marshall and George Patton.

WHERE TO STAY

Holiday Inn Express
US 11, 880 N Lee Hwy
Lexington, VA 24450
800-315-2621, 540-463-7351
$$ ✕ ▣

Country Inn & Suites
875 N Lee Hwy on US 11
Lexington, VA 24450
540-464-9000
$$-$$$ ⚓ ▣

Historic Country Inns of Lexington
11 N Main Street
Lexington, VA 24450
540-463-2044
$$$$ ☕

CAMPING

Longs Campground
82 Camprgound Lane
5 miles W of Lexington on Rt 39.
540-463-7672

**Mallard Duck Camping
& Bike Hostel**
2741 S River Rd
Vesuvius, VA 24483
540-261-5128
Outside of Lexington .5 miles N
of CR 608/ CR 603 junction. 40
miles from the Gap. 9 miles from
Lexington.

Tye River Gap Recreation Area
28.7 miles from the Gap.
Store and camping.

FOOD AND DINING

Food In Route:
Plan on having breakfast before
heading out and be sure to stock
up on lunch supplies. The first
real food stop is 44 miles at the
South River Market. Tye River
Gap Campground before Vesuvius
has camp store. There is no food
in Vesuvius.

Lexington Coffee Company
Lexington, VA 24450
Fresh brew downtown.

Applebee's Restaurant
870 N Lee Hwy
Lexington, VA 24450
On US 11 near Holiday Inn Express
and Country Inns & Suites.

SPECIAL INTEREST

Blue Ridge Parkway
2551 Mountain View Rd
Vinton, WA 24179
828-271-4779

Created in the 1930s by the CCC,
the Blue Ridge Parkway was the
nation's first rural parkway and is
also the nation's longest, covering
469 scenic miles. Handcrafted
stone walls, split-rail fences,
hickory and oak trees, azaleas and
rhododendrons line the roadway.

**Virginia Military Institute
& Museum– VMI**
Jackson Memorial Hall
415 Letcher A   ve
Lexington, VA 24450
540-464-7334
www.marshallfoundation.org/
museum/
General George Marshall
Museum.

**Lee Chapel and Museum
– National Historic Landmark**
Washington & Lee University
240 W Washington Street
Lexington, VA 24450
540-458-8768
General Robert E. Lee burial site.

Stonewall Jackson House
8 E Washington Street
Lexington, VA 24450
540-463-2552
www.stonewalljackson.org
Guided tours daily.

Virginia Horse Center
Route 39
487 Maury River Rd
Lexington, VA 24450
540-463-2194
www.horsecenter.org

Lexington & Rockbridge Area Visitor Center
106 E Washington Street
Lexington, VA 24450
540-463-3777
www.lexingtonvirginia.com

Travel Shenandoah - Virginia 511
800-578-4111
www.travelshenandoah.com

Lexington Bike Shop
130 S Main
Lexington, VA 24450
540-463-7969

Today you'll pass by burbling creeks and streams, marmots, purple irises and peonies. Down the road, the Appalachian Trail crosses the freeway where you may run across a hardy hiker and be thankful that you're on a bike. If you're looking for a detour (at about 17 miles) and general tourist amusement, visit the "Natural Bridge." Thomas Jefferson purchased the 250-foot-high natural stone bridge in 1783, declaring it the Seventh Wonder of the World. It's a wonder that so many visit it, but it's out in the middle of nowhere and does make for an entertaining diversion. There is a very friendly Ranger Station at the Tourist Center.

PLACES TO STAY

Comfort Inn
2545 Lee Hwy
Troutville, VA 24175
866-365-9867, 540-992-5600
$$ 🛏🏊

Howard Johnson
437 Roanoke Road
Daleville, VA 26083
800-330-8707, 540-992-1234
$$🛏🏊

Holiday Inn Express
3200 Lee Hwy S
Troutville, VA 24175
540-966-4444
$$ 🛏🏊

CAMPING

Natural Bridge KOA
214 Kildeer Lane
Natural Bridge, VA 24578
Off route 6 miles.
540-291-2770

Troutville City Park
Hwy 11
Town clerk: 540-992-4401
Behind the Thriftway by Town Hall.

Camp Bethel
328 Bethel Rd
Fincastle, VA 24090
540-992-2940
Junction of CR 606. 9 miles before Troutville.
www.bethelvirginia.org

FOOD AND DINING

TA Truck Stop

Taco Time

Cracker Barrel

SPECIAL INTEREST

Natural Bridge Tourist Center
800-533-1414, 540-291-2121
"The most sublime of nature's
works" (Thomas Jefferson). Once
owned by Thomas Jefferson, the
Natural Bridge is on the National
Register of Historic Places.
www.naturalbridgeva.com

RESOURCES

Botetourt Chamber
540-473-8280
www.bot-co-chamber.com

Roanoke Valley Visitor Center
101 Shenandoah Ave NE
Roanoke, VA 24011
800-635-5535, 540-342-6025
www.visitroanokeva.com

DAY 8 TROUTVILLE TO CHRISTIANSBURG
Pop: 15,000
Mileage: 47
Est. Elevation: 2,500
AC Map: 12:140, 139

The first eight to nine miles are an obstacle course just getting out of town. You'll share the road with trucks on their way to Roanoke Cement Company at Botetourt Landfill. Once you get past the landfill at 12 miles, the ride becomes more rural. The scenery in Catawba Valley and the North Fork of Roanoke River are reminiscent of the gentle English countryside. Christiansburg is a speck of history surrounded by a new shopping center. The town square commemorates a duel that occurred before the Revolutionary War.

PLACES TO STAY

The Oaks Victorian Inn
311 East Main Street
Christiansburg, VA 24073
540-381-1500
www.theoaksvictorianinn.com
$$$$ ☊
AAA, 4-diamond.

Evergreen Bell Capozzi House B&B
201 E Main Street
Christiansburg, VA 24073
540-382-7372
$$$ ☊≋

Econo Lodge
2430 Roanoke
Christiansburg, VA 24073
540-382-6161. 855-499-0001
$$ ☊≋

Four Pines Hostel
6164 Newport Rd
Catawba, VA 24070
1.7 miles off-route from junction of route and SR 311
540-309-8615

Hampton Inn
380 Arbor Drive
Christiansburg, VA 24068
888-370-0981, 540-381-5874
$$$ ☊≋▣

Super 8 Motel
2780 Roanoke Street
Christiansburg, VA 24073
800-536-0367, 540-382-7421

CAMPING

Interstate Overnight Park
2705 Roanoke Street
Christiansburg, VA 24073
540-382-1554
2.5 miles off route.

FOOD & DINING

Macado Restaurant
19 W Main Street, Downtown
540-381-8872
Christiansburg, VA 24073

There are numerous food spots in the burbs.

SPECIAL INTEREST

Montgomery Museum and Lewis Miller Regional Center
300 S Pepper Street
Christiansburg, VA 24073
540-382-5644
Civil War memorabilia in 1850 historic house.

RESOURCES

East Coasters Bike Shop
1301 N Main Street
Blackburg, VA 24060
540-951-2369
www.eastcoasters.com

Christiansburg & Montgomery County Chamber
1520 N Franklin St
Christiansburg, VA 24073
540-382-3020
www.montgomerycc.org

NEARBY RESOURCES

IN ROANOKE, OFF ROUTE, 8 MILES SE OF CATAWBA.

Cardinal Bicycle
2901 Orange Avenue
Roanoke, VA 24012
540-344-2453

East Coasters Cycle & Fitness
3544 Electric Road
Roanoke, VA 24018
540-774-7933

Today's ride leads to Wytheville between the Blue Ridge and Allegheny Mountains. Christiansburg is an old town now being displaced by suburbs on the way to Blacksburg. Newburg at 23 miles is charming but, as of this writing, there's no food; so just keep peddling to JW's Quickstop Bait & Tackle at 25.5 miles just beyond the Clayton Marina.

PLACES TO STAY

Hampton Inn
950 Peppers Ferry Road
Wytheville, VA 24382
276-228-6090, 888-370-0981
$$$ 🢁 ≋

Ramada Inn
955 Peppers Ferry Road
Wytheville, VA 24382
276-228-6000
$$ 🢁 ≋

Super 8 Motel
130 Nye Circle
Wytheville, VA 24382
800-454-3213, 276-228-6620
$-$$

CAMPING

KOA Campground
231 KOA Road
Wytheville, VA 24382
800-562-3380, 276-228-2601
Left at 38.3 miles. 4.5 E of town.

Elizabeth Brown Memorial Park
250 54th St
Wytheville, VA 24832
276-223-3378
Check in at Community Center.

FOOD & DINING

Unlimited choices, including all fast food chains in Wytheville.

Applebee's Neighborhood Bar & Grill
1440 E Main Street
Wytheville, VA 24382
276-223-4404
Always reliable.

Peking Restaurant
105 Main Drive
Wytheville, VA 24382
276-228-5515
Good Chinese veggies.

SPECIAL INTEREST

Wytheville Historic Walking Tour
Wytheville Convention and
Visitors Bureau
150 E Monroe Street
Wytheville, VA 24382
877-347-8307, 276-223-3355
www.visitwytheville.com
www.wytheville.org

RESOURCES

**Blue Ridge Highlands Visitor
Center**
150 E Monroe Street
Wytheville, VA 24382
276-223-3355

The New Wheel Bike Shop
1220 E Main Street
Redford, VA 24141
540-731-1211

Which way to Louisa?

The day starts at the Wytheville City Hall where you'll head out of town toward US 11, which for several miles is a four-lane road lined by manicured lawns. Slowly the four lanes become two, and you'll be on the West Lee Highway S11, traveling through cattle and goat farms. At 22 miles you'll see the Summit Missionary Church, "revivals available." At 28 miles you'll enter the Rogers National Recreation Area and spend the rest of the day on the Rogers Scenic Byway, passing numerous burbling creeks. Look for the 25 flavors of ice cream and soft serve at the Mountain View Food Mart along the route. At 43 miles, stop at the Laurel Valley Log House Community Church, built with log pews. The day ends in Damascus, called "The friendliest town on the Appalachian Trail."

PLACES TO STAY

Lazy Fox Inn
133 Imboden Street
Damascus, VA 24236
276-475-5838
www.lazyfoxinn.com

CAMPING

"The Place"
200 E Laurel Ave
Damascus, VA 24236
276-475-3441
Hostel off Laurel behind Damascus Methodist Church.

Iron Horse Campground
30460 Blossom Road
Damascus, VA 24236
276-492-9689
2 miles west of Damascus on US E8.

FOOD & DINING

Food In Route:

Sugar Grove Diner
1424 N Main Street
Marion, VA 24354
276-782-3351
25 miles from Wytheville.

Mountain View Food Mart
5225 Sugar Grove Hwy
Sugar Grove, VA 24375
276-672-3037
25 flavors ice cream and soft serve.

Weaver's Grocery
6315 Whitetop Rd
Troutdale, VA 24378
276-388-3415
Famous Whitetop Burger,
ingredients are a trade secret in
Konnarock, 12.5 miles from
Troutdale.

Baja Cafe
103 N Shady Lane
Damascus, VA 24236
276-475-6005

Mojoe's Cafe
331 Douglas Street
Damascus, VA 24236
276-475-5505
Great for coffee and wifi.

SPECIAL INTEREST

The Creeper Trail
Begun as an Indian footpath and
used by Daniel Boone, it was part
of the Virginia-Carolina Railroad
from Abington to Damascus. Got
its nickname from the locomotives
that crept up the steep grades.
Now 34.3 miles of unpaved road.
The Bike Station takes rental bikes
to the top for a delightful ride
down to Damascus.

Abington Convention/Visitor's Bureau,
335 Cummings Street
Abington, VA 24210
800-435-3440, 276-676-2282

Appalachian Trail Day in May
Damascus Town Hall
540-475-3831

RESOURCES

Mt. Rogers Outfitters
110 W Laurel Ave
Damascus, VA 34236
276-475-5416
Free Internet.

The Bike Station
501 E 3rd Street
Damascus, VA 24236
276-475-3629
www.thebikestation.net
Bike rentals only.

Adventure Damascus & Bike Shop
128 W Laurel Avenue
Damascus, VA 24236
888-595-BIKE (2453)
276-475-6262
www.adventuredamascus.com

Sundog Outfitters
331 Douglas Drive
Damascus, VA 24236
276-475-6252

Blue Blaze Bike & Shuttle Service
226 W Laurel Avenue
Damascus, VA 24236
276-475-5095

This is the most difficult uphill on the route thus far; so we personally decided not to go to Breaks in one day. You'll follow the Holston River for the first 10 miles. At 14 miles is Miller's Deli Market for "Broasted" Chicken. At about 25 miles there is a 3.7- mile climb of eight to nine percent grade, the longest, hardest climb so far. Many cyclists stay in the church at Elk Garden and bike into Rosedale for food, unless the church has supplies, which sometimes they do. Rosedale is only 2 miles from Elk Garden.

CAMPING

Same as above. Only Option.

FOOD & DINING

Food In Route, see:
www.virginia.org/Cities/Rosedale/

PLACES TO STAY

ELK GARDEN - Church
540-889-8041
No shower. Restrooms only, sleep on carpeted floor. Kitchen is often stocked with donated food.

Elk Garden United Methodist Church

You'll find yourself on a busy two-lane highway on the way to Breaks. Unfortunately, it's the only way to get to the park. There are many trucks, and it's "red neck" country. Indeed, it is a dangerous road. However, the route does quiet down after Council (about 14 miles out of Rosedale) and there are numerous food stops along the way.

Council has a little park along the river with an old steam engine, picnic tables and a log cabin. You'll ride through several other small towns like Davenport and Birchleaf and the larger Haysi at 32 miles full of coal and logging trucks. You'll make virtually no turns during the whole day, staying on Route 80 all the way to the Park entrance at about 39 miles.

PLACES TO STAY

Rhododendron Restaurant & Conference Center
Breaks Interstate Park
Breaks, VA 24607
800-982-5122, 276-865-4413
www.breakspark.com
$$ ☂ ✕

Gateway Motel
On Route 80
2307 Breaks Park Rd
Breaks, VA 24607
276-531-8481
$
2 miles downhill from Breaks Park. Pizza and grocery across from Gateway Motel.

John W. Moore Motel
494 Main Street
Elkhorn City, KY 41522
606-754-8017
$
7 miles downhill from Breaks Park.

CAMPING

Breaks Interstate Park
627 Commission Circle
Breaks, VA 24607
800-933-PARK (7275)
www.breakspark.com

FOOD & DINING

**Rhododendron Restaurant
& Conference Center**
Breaks Interstate Park
Breaks, VA 24607
800-982-5122, 276-865-4413
Peach pie a la mode and chocolate
sundaes.

Rusty Fork Café
105 Patty Loveless Drive
Elkhorn, KY 41522
606-754-4494
Local hangout 6.4 miles downhill
from the Lodge.

SPECIAL INTEREST

Breaks Interstate Park
Breaks, VA 24607
800-982-5122, 276-865-4413
www.breakspark.com
The park fills up completely
during Memorial and Labor Day
weekends. Book in advance.
Lodge, cottages, campground,
swimming pool, pedal boats,
mountain bike rentals, hiking,
white-water rafting.

KENTUCKY
9 Days - 506 Miles

Kentucky is one of the most fascinating of all the states along the TransAm route. The people in Appalachia, often with the least to share, share the most. Riding from Virginia across Kentucky to Missouri is a history lesson in humanity and the survival of a proud people in a mostly rural setting. Birthplace of Abraham Lincoln, the state is a wonderful combination of early pioneers like Daniel Boone, struggling coal miners, bluegrass music, gentlemen farmers, tobacco and corn and, of course, Kentucky bourbon. "My Old Kentucky Home," by Stephen Foster expresses the mood perfectly.

This is a hilly state and, as rumored among cyclists, there are lots of stray dogs. A simple whistle around your neck will solve a multitude of problems with the pesky pups. When all else fails, try the Sabre!

KENTUCKY FACTS & RESOURCES

Fast Facts
Population: 3.9 million
Capital: Frankfort
Nickname: Bluegrass State
Flower: Goldenrod
Bird: Kentucky Cardinal

Key Dates in History
1774   Harrodsburg- First settlement
1792   Kentucky statehood

Department of Travel
PO Box 2011
Capital Plaza Tower, 22nd Flr
500 Mero Street
Frankfort, KY 40602
800-225-8747
www.kentuckytourism.com

DAY 13 BREAKS TO HINDMAN, KY
Pop: 763
Mileage: 70
Est. Elevation: 3,500-4,000
AC Map: 11:133, 132, 131

Start the morning with a long descent from Breaks Interstate Park into Kentucky. At 3.4 miles you'll cross the Kentucky state line. Today's ride goes through the heart of Appalachia coal country. You'll be traveling on two-lane roads and one four-lane road with a wide shoulder. It's a long, tough day, perhaps the hardest of the trip with minimal accommodations.

A study in contrasts, you'll see poverty, beer shacks, $100,000 coal trucks parked in the front of $10,000 trailer homes, empty grocery stores and friendly folks.

The Pippa Passes Hostel (62 miles) is located near the Alice Lloyd College. At 70 miles from Breaks just outside of Hindman there is the 80 Motel. Currently there is no open motel in Hindman itself. Check with Knott County Chamber for an update, 606-785-0223.

PLACES TO STAY

Knott County Historical Society B&B
Hindman, KY 41822
606-785-5751
Also offers camping to cyclists.

CAMPING

Hindman Settlement School
147 Carew Drive
Hindman, KY 41822
606-785-5475
Limited camping by permission.
Call for Sam Linkous.

FOOD & DINING

FOOD IN ROUTE:

Rusty Fork Cafe
105 Patty Loveless Dr.
Elkhorn City, KY
606-754-4494
7 miles from Breaks.

Alice Lloyd College
100 Purpose Road
Pippa Passes, KY 41844
606-368-6000
ww.alc.edu
Four-year private liberal arts
college established by pioneer
Alice Lloyd. Possible dorm
rooms available only by calling in
advance. Jim & Joe Stebb

Knott County Tourism
30 Bailey Street
Hindman, KY 41822
606-785-5881

Note: If you stopped at Pippa Passes, mileage is 51 to Buckhorn Lake and 73.5 to Booneville.

After yesterday's hilly ride, you'll be happy with the relatively flat start today. Gentle roads roll along Troublesome Creek, also the name of the local newspaper. Soaring sandstone cliffs show coal veins. Once you get outside Hazard the road begins to buck like a bronco but by now you're used to that feeling. Around 18 miles a whole series of cemeteries (John Turner, Bob Turner, Warren Turner) remind you of family life in Kentucky. Buckhorn Lake State Park is four miles downhill to the lovely campground and lodge. Do not go there unless you are staying the night (or craving more hills). If you're feeling strong, you can skip Buckhorn Lake Resort and continue on to Booneville. Buckhorn Lake turnoff to Booneville adds another 1,500 feet of elevation to the day.

PLACES TO STAY

BUCKHORN
Buckhorn Lake State Resort Park
4441 Kentucky Highway 1833
Buckhorn, KY 41721
800-325-0059, 800-255-7275
606-398-7510
$$ ✕ ≋ ◻
Reservations are taken at the Lodge up to three years in advance. No reservations needed for camping.

CAMPING

Buckhorn Lake State Resort Park
4441 Kentucky Highway 1833
Buckhorn, KY 41721
800-325-0059
www.reserveamerica.com

Buckhorn Lake Campground
.5 miles S of Buckhorn on SR 1387
606-398-7250, 877-444-6777
www.recreation.gov

FOOD & DINING

Buckhorn Lake State Resort Park
The only restaurant in the area.

SPECIAL INTEREST

"The Log Cathedral"
Buckhorn, KY 41721
Church built out of logs in 1928.

PLACES TO STAY

BOONEVILLE

Linda's Victorian Rose B&B
496 Kentucky / Hwy 30
Booneville, KY 41314
606-593-7662
Email:
victorianrosebb@hotmail.com
$$ ✕
2 miles out of Booneville. Linda
is the unofficial Director of
Hospitality for the area and does a
super job.

CAMPING

Linda's Victorian Rose B&B
496 KY 30
Booneville, KY 41314
606-593-7662
Email:
victorianrosebb@hotmail.com

Bike Hostel Pavilion
Booneville Methodist Church
40 Mulberry Street
Booneville, KY 41314
606-593-6561
Four blocks from downtown.

FOOD & DINING

Shopwise Supermarket
279 KY 28
Booneville, KY 41314
606-593-7308
Great pizza to go.

Dooley's Diner
Court Street
Boonevill, KY 41314
606-593-5270
Good and inexpensive!

Booneville is in a dry county. No
beer or alcohol sold anywhere.

SPECIAL INTEREST

If you are staying at Linda's
Victorian B&B, stop at Shopwise
grocery in Booneville and pick up
a pizza or food supplies.

Linda A. Moore Marcum, Director of Hospitality

Editor's note: There's a new, better route from Bighill to Vincent since we did the trip. Maps are updated.

You'll roll through horse country today on your way to Berea, a cultured, arts and crafts, and college town. Along the route swarms of butterflies will greet you in a typical Appalachian hollow. At 4 miles you'll pass the Appalachian Fireside Crafts shop. Deer, red fox and possums abound. Big backyard gardens grow tempting vegetables unfortunately rarely seen at the many all-you-can eat buffet restaurants. You may pass Knob Lick Church, then Gravel Lick Road, then Red Lick Baptist Church. There sure are a lot of licks in this day, but it makes not a lick of sense to us!

Note: If you don't get all the way to Booneville on Day 14, instead of going to Berea you may wish to stop in Irvine at 56 miles.

PLACES TO STAY

Boone Tavern Hotel
100 Main Street
Berea, KY 40404
800-366-9358, 859-985-3700
$$$$ ✕
Historic Hotel of America

America's Best Value Inn
196 Prince Royal Drive
Berea, KY 40404
859-986-8426, 888-315-2378
$$ ☕

Holiday Motel
100 Jane Street
Berea, KY 40404
859-986-9311
$ 🌊

CAMPING

Oh! Kentucky Campground
562 Paint Lick Road
Berea, KY 40461
859-986-1150

Walnut Meadow Campground
711 Paint Lick Road
Berea, KY 40461
859-986-6180

FOOD & DINING

Food In Route:

Berea Coffee and Tea Co.
124 S Main Street
Berea, KY 40403
859-986-7656
Downtown Berea
Great spot and offers wifi.

Numerous places on College Square.

SPECIAL INTEREST

Berea is designated "the folk arts and crafts capital of Kentucky."

Berea College Log House Craft Gallery
200 Estrill Street
Berea, KY 40403
859-985-3225

Berea College
College Square
101 Chestnut Street
Berea, KY 40403
859-985-3000
The Appalachian College Foundation helps Appalachian students attend the private Berea College, founded in 1855.

RESOURCES

The Morning Glory Bed & Bath
140 N Broadway
Berea, KY 40404
859-986-8661
Welcomes bicyclists.

Berea Tourist & Convention Commission
204 N Broadway
Berea, KY 40403
859-986-2540
www.berea.com

DAY 16 BEREA TO HARRODSBURG, KY
Pop: 7,954
Mileage: 46
Est. Elevation: 1,500
AC Map: 10:127,126

This is the start of Daniel Boone and bluegrass country. You'll see blankets of honeysuckle and cattle ranches and ride through 45 miles of horse heaven. Look for tall Shaker-style barns made of long boards. There are several nice coffee stops along the way and many antique shops. At 39 miles you'll pass Lake Herrington, scene of numerous summer bass tournaments. Stop at 43 miles and say "Hi" to the folks at the Village Inn in Burgin, "the friendliest little city in America."

PLACES TO STAY

Beaumont Inn
638 Beaumont Inn Drive
Harrodsburg, KY 40330
800-352-3992, 859-734-3381
www.beaumontinn.com
$$$ ▱ ✕ ♨
National Register of Historic Places. Off Main Street.

Country Hearth Inn
105 Commercial Drive
Harrodsburg, KY 40330
888-294-6492, 859-734-2400
$$ ▱

CAMPING

Cummins Ferry Campground & Marina
2558 Cummins Ferry Road
Harrodsburg, KY 40330
859-865-2003

Chimney Rock RV Park & Campground
220 Chimney Rock Road
Harrodsburg, KY 40330
859-748-5252
8 miles before Harrodsburg.

FOOD & DINING

Food In Route:

Village Inn Restaurant
501 E Main Street
Burgin, KY 40175
859-748-5943
(5 miles from Harrodsburg).
Try the Mooney Burger or lemon
meringue pie.

In Harrodsburg
Numerous fast food and
restaurants.

RESOURCES

**Harrodsburg/Mercer County
Tourist Commission**
488 Price Avenue
Harrodsburg, KY 40330
859-734-2364. 800-355-9192

Chamber of Commerce
131 N Chiles Street
Harrodsburg, KY 40330
859-734-2365

SPECIAL INTEREST

Old Fort Harrod State Park
100 S College Street
Harrodsburg, KY 40330
KY Departament of Parks
859-734-3314, 800-255-7275
First settlement in Kentucky
by James Harrod, 1774.

Dog days of Kentucky

Gentle, rolling hills dotted with tobacco plants and white fences take you to Bardstown, "the bourbon capital of the world," and Kentucky's second oldest town. At 31.5 miles you'll pass the Lincoln Homestead Park and later at 45 miles the Bluegrass Highway. Bardstown is a good place for a layover day. This historic town, with Stephen Foster's My Old Kentucky Home State Park, has excellent accommodations, ice cream parlors, drug stores, a great tourist information center with video and much more. The Bardstown Library across from the Talbott Tavern has free internet access.

PLACES TO STAY

Arbor Rose B&B
209 Stephen Foster Avenue
Bardstown, KY 40004
888-828-3330, 502-349-0014
$$$ ⎁
Voted Best B&B in Kentucky.

Bardstown Parkview Motel
418 E Stephen Foster Avenue
Bardstown, KY 40004
800-732-2384, 502-348-5983
$$ ⎁ ≊

Jailer's Inn
111 W Stephen Foster Avenue
Bardstown, KY 40004
800-948-5551, 502-348-5551
www.jailersinn.com
$$ ⎁
"A captivating experience"

Old Talbott Tavern & Inn
107 W Stephen Foster Avenue
Court Square
Bardstown, KY 40004
800-4-TAVERN, 502-348-3494
www.talbotts.com
$$ ⎁ ✕

CAMPING

My Old Kentucky Home Campground/ White Acres
501 E Stephen Foster Ave
Hwy 49 off Hwy 245
Bardstown, KY 40004
800-323-7803, 502-348-3502
One mile E on US 150 off
Bluegrass Parkway.

FOOD & DINING

Old Talbott Tavern & Inn
107 W Stephen Foster Ave
Court Square
Bardstown, KY 40004
800-4-TAVERN
www.talbotts.com
Bourbon-glazed carrots and steaks.

Kurtz Restaurant
418 E Stephen Foster Ave
Bardstown, KY 40004
502-348-8964
Local favorite.

Many other restaurants and small delis.

SPECIAL INTEREST

Ninety percent of the nation's bourbon is produced in Kentucky. Bardstown was voted second most popular destination in Kentucky. "My Old Kentucky Home" was written here by Stephen Foster. Walking Tour of Historic Bardstown.
Annual Bourbon Festival if you time it right.

RESOURCES

Bardstown Visitor Center
800-638-4877
www.bardstowntourism.com

This is a short day and the miles go easily. Right out of Bardstown 1.3 miles is the Heaven Hill Distillery with tastings. Yesterday's tobacco fields have turned to corn. Horses race up to the fences as you peddle by their pastures. The route is as gentle as the countryside. At 26.5 miles you'll pass through Howard's Town with a little store - no, not named for my husband. Today's roadside attractions include the site of Lincoln's birthplace and boyhood home and Thomas Lincoln's (Abe's dad's) original homesite. Accommodations at the end of the day are sketchy. Check out the Lincoln Jamboree, live country western music on Friday and Saturday nights.

PLACES TO STAY

Cabin Fever II B&B
3030 Old Elisabethtown Road
Hodgenville, KY 42748
270-358-4415
One room, 3 miles out of town
$

Cabins across from Birthplace.
Call Carl Howell:
270-358-3626

CAMPING

LaRue County Park
200 City Park Road
Hodgenville, KY 42748
270-358-9261
Behind High School at US 31 and Lincoln Blvd.

Jamboree Camping
Behind the theater and stage. Free camping with Jamboree ticket.

FOOD & DINING

Several places in downtown Hodgenville. Just out of town, Lincoln Jamboree has big buffet.

Lincoln Jamboree
2579 Lincoln Farm Road
Hodgenville, KY 42748
270-358-3545
"Kentucky's #1 Country Music Showplace."

Lincoln Museum
66 Lincoln Square
Hodgenville, KY 42748
270-358-3163

**Abraham Lincoln Birthplace
National Historic Site**
2995 Lincoln Farm Road
US 31 and KY 61
Hodgenville, KY 42748
270-358-3137
3 miles S of Hodgenville.

Lincoln's Boyhood Home
7120 Bardstown Rd
Hodgenville, KY 42748
270-358-3137
Open daily.

**LaRue County Chamber of
Commerce**
60 Lincoln Square
Hodgenville, KY 42748
270-358-3137
www.laruecountychamber.org

The first 20 miles are some of the flattest on the entire trip. Now cattle ranches outnumber the horse farms as you pass Amish homes nestled far back from the road. You'll notice an absence of power lines, and road signs depict horse and buggies. Birds and butterflies seem to follow the route with red-winged blackbirds, hawks, yellow finches and blue birds making an occasional appearance. The day ends at the 637-acre park which boasts a laundry, restaurants, rooms, camping, nine-hole golf course, fishing, swimming and small airstrip for private planes. Groceries are available outside the park.

PLACES TO STAY

Rough River Dam State Resort Park
450 - I6 - 1003
Falls of Rough, KY 40119
270-257-2311, 800-325-1713
$$ ✕ 🏊 ⬛

Pine Tree Inn
13689 Falls of Rough Road
Hwy 70 across from park.
Falls of Rough, KY 40119
270-257-2771
$ 🏊

CAMPING

Rough River Dam State Resort Park
450 Lodge Road
Falls of Rough, KY 40119
270-257-2311, 800-325-1713

FOOD & DINING

The resort has a dining room. There are several small gas station/grocery stores nearby.

SPECIAL INTEREST

Rough River Dam State Resort Park
Boating, fishing, golf, nature trails, swimming.

This is another short day. Your bike route will continue through rural countryside heading towards Kentucky's third largest town, Owensboro. At 16.7 miles you'll pass Jumping Jack's Market. At 27 miles in Whitesville at a junction with SR 764, our recommended route goes off the Adventure Cycling map and leads you to Owensboro. The AC route turns left on SR 764 towards Utica. If you're going to Owensboro, you continue straight on SR 54. At 43.5 miles make a left on an unsigned inconspicuous 18th Street to bypass downtown. At 46 miles turn left on Fredericka at a T intersection in front of Owensboro High School to find numerous motels.

PLACES TO STAY

Hampton Inn
615 Salem Drive
Owensboro, KY 42303
270-926-2006, 888-370-0981
$$ 🛏🏊

Fairfield Inn Marriott
800 Salem Drive
Owensboro, KY 42303
270-688-8887
$$ 🛏🏊

Motel 6
4585 Frederica Street
Owensboro, KY 42301
270-686-8606
$ 🛏

CAMPING

English Park
1530 McJohnson Ave
Owensboro, KY 42303
Owensboro Parks & Recreation
270-687-8718
Call first.

FOOD & DINING

Moonlight Bar-B-Q
2840 W Parish Avenue
Owensboro, KY 42303
270-684-8143
Best barbecue.

Many options available near
motels and in downtown
Owensboro.

SPECIAL INTEREST

International Barbecue Festival
270-926-6938
Second weekend in May.
www.bbqfest.com

**International Bluegrass Music
Museum**
207 E 2nd Street
Owensboro, KY 42303
270-926-7891
Riverpark Center.

RESOURCES

**Owensboro County Tourist
Commission**
Visitor Center
215 E 2nd Street (US 60)
Owensboro, KY 42303
800-489-1131, 270-426-1100
www.visitowensboro.com

Quality Bike Shop
1728 Sweeney Street
Owensboro, KY 42303
270-691-9460

DAY 21 OWENSBORO TO PROVIDENCE, KY
Pop: 3,320
Mileage: 61.5   Est. Elevation: 1,500
AC Map: 10:120,119

If you are departing from Owensboro, head toward Utica on US 431 with flat roads, wide shoulders and some traffic. At Utica, make a right on SR 140 to rejoin the AC route. More rolling hills will take you past the Perdue Chicken plant in Sebree, which has a distinct chicken odor. At 48 miles in Dixon, the site of the Webster County Courthouse named for Daniel Webster, the AC route goes straight on SR 132 towards Marion, a total distance of about 80 miles. We recommend making a left on US 41 Alt at Dixon and a right on SR 120 into Providence at about 61.5 miles (10 miles from Dixon).

The end of the day flattens out as you get closer to Providence, the remains of a coal-mining town that still has a Coal Festival complete with a most-beautiful-baby contest but limited accommodations.

PLACES TO STAY

For nearby motels/hotels, see:
www.yellowpages.com/
providence-ky/hotels

CAMPING

**Providence High School/
Elementary School**
Call Debby Gooch at Magnolia House 270-667-2642
or Jerry Fritz, Providence City Office 270-667-5463
E-mail: providence@kih.net

Sebree Spring Park
Hwy 132 via Sebree
Roger Powell Road
Sebree, KY
35 miles from Owensboro

Marion City/County Park
Old Shady Grove Road
Marion, KY 42064
Half mile off route.
Check with police. 80 miles from Owensboro.

FOOD & DINING

Food In Route:

O.T.'s Inc.
535 US Hwy 41A5
Dixon, KY 42409
270-639-9446
Named after Oscar Theopolis,
longtime local circuit court judge,
who owned the site in 1905. O.T.'s
reputedly has the best turkey-
stacked sandwiches in the state.

Several small grocery stores and
restaurants in Providence.

SPECIAL INTEREST

Providence Coal Festival
Cutest baby contest.

Greens Farms General Store
National Register of Historic
Places. On route, now a museum.

Kentucky horsepower

The Ohio River.

ILLINOIS
4 Days - 134 Miles

The shortest crossing of any state on the route, you travel only 133 miles across the southern tip of Illinois. You'll pass through the Illinois Ozarks and the Shawnee National Forest before entering Missouri. Plan on a stop in Carbondale, where bike shops abound and internet access is available at the Southern Illinois University, coal-powered of course.

ILLINOIS FACTS & RESOURCES

Fast Facts
Population: 12.1 million
Capital: Springfield
Nickname: Land of Lincoln
Flower: Violet
Bird: Cardinal
Tree: White Oak

Key Dates in History
1673   French Missionaries settle in Illinois country

1818   Enters Union (21st State)

1860   Abraham Lincoln becomes president

Illinois Bureau of Tourism
100 W Randolph, Chicago, IL 60601
800-2CONNECT, 312-874-4732
www.enjoyillinois.com

Southern IllinoisTourism Info
www.southernillinoistourism.org

Tourism Bureau Southwestern Illinois
800-442-1488, 618-257-1488
www.thetourismbureau.org

Leaving Providence just continue on SR 120 to intersect with SR 132 and rejoin the AC route to Marion. This is Amish Country. Before crossing the Ohio River, stop at Yoder's Variety Store in Marion, KY (about 20 miles from Providence). You'll see fresh fruit stands, wild roses and fields of yellow day lilies along the route. The state line is the Ohio River, where you'll take a short ride on an open-air ferry to reach Missouri. We were sad to leave Kentucky. Near the Ferry landing on the Illinois side is Cave Rock State Park where pirates once preyed on unsuspecting river travelers. (not bicyclists however!)

PLACES TO STAY

River Rose Inn B&B
1 Main Street
Elizabethtown, IL 62931
618-287-8811
www.shaneelink.com/riverose
$$$ 🍵🏊
On the Ohio River across from the Old Rose Hotel.

Old Rose Hotel
92 Main Street
Elizabethtown, IL 62931
618-287-2872
$$ 🍵
National Historic Hotel on Ohio River, now run by the state.

Cave-In Rock State Park
1 New State Park Road
Cave-In Rock, IL 62919
618-289-4545
$$ 🍴
4 duplex cabins. 10 miles east of Elizabethtown.

CAMPING

Cave-In Rock State Park & Restaurant
Cave In Rock, IL 62919
618-289-4545
$$ 🍴
10 miles east of Elizabethtown on Ohio River by ferry landing.

Dixon Springs State Park
10 miles W of Golconda on SR 146, highly recommended.
Golconda, IL 62938
616-949-3394

Tower Rock Campground
Shawnee National Forest
618-253-7114
4 miles east of Elizabethtown on
route, off 146th.

FOOD & DINING

E Town River Restaurant
Front Street
Elizabethtown, IL 62931
618-287-2333
A houseboat tied to the banks of
the river, specializing in catfish.

Town & Country Restaurant
Elizabethtown, IL 62931
618-287-2611
Local color.

Reeds C Store
Behind Town and Country, open
24 hours

PLACES TO STAY

GOLCONDA Pop: 800

Michael's Motel
Adams Street
Golconda, IL 62938
618-683-2424
$

CAMPING

GOLCONDA

Deer Run Campground
Route 3
Golconda, IL 62938
618-683-8410
Check in town for directions.

Ohio River Recreation Area
R.R. 2
Rauchfuss Hill Campground
on 146th in town
Golconda, IL 62938
618-276-4405

SPECIAL INTEREST

Golconda Marina
Golconda IL 62938
618-683-5875

RESOURCES

**Golconda Chamber of
Commerce**
206 Main Street
Golconda, IL 62938
618-683-9702

Hardin County Tourism
618-683-6246

Shawnee National Forest
Elizabethtown Ranger District
800-699-6637,
800-MY-WOODS,
618-253-7114

DAY 23 ELIZABETHTOWN TO VIENNA, IL
Pop: 1,500 (off route, on AC map)
Mileage: 40
Est. Elevation: 1,500
AC Map: 10:117, 116

You'll travel on gentle, rolling hills on a wonderful, wide two-lane road today all the way to Vienna. This segment goes off the official AC Route but stays on the AC map. At 13 miles, instead of making the AC right at Eddyville Road, stay on SR 146, continuing to Vienna. According to the residents, Golconda, which you pass at 16 miles, has the biggest deer population in Illinois. Look for the many wood ducks in the Cyprus Swamps of the Shawnee National Forest. The route goes by several Illinois correctional facilities. There's a chocolate factory in Dixon Springs 10 miles beyond Golconda for the best chocolate on the trip as well as excellent homemade ice cream. The Vienna City Park is the site of one of the stopping points of the Cherokee Nation encampment along the famous Trail of Tears. Headquarters for the 45-mile Tunnel Hill State Trail are located in Vienna, one of only two established bike trails in the state of Illinois.

PLACES TO STAY

Hotel 7 Inn Vienna
Junction I-24 & Hwy 146
709 E Vine Street
Vienna, IL 62995
www.booking.com
$$ ⊘ ☂

Country Schemes B&B
3220 Old Metropolis Rd.
Vienna, IL 62995
618-658-9044

CAMPING

Ferne Clyffe State Park
90 Office Drive
Hwy 37
Goreville, IL 62939
618-995-2411
Approximately 13 miles beyond
Vienna on SR 37.

Cedar Lake Campground
2090 Gilead Church Road
off Hwy 45
Vienna, IL 62995
618-695-2600
Private campground, 3-4 miles
out of town.

Vienna Carnegie Public Library
401 Poplar Street
Vienna, IL 62995
618-658-5051
Built in 1910 on Main Square.
Has one computer. Closed on
Thursdays.

FOOD & DINING

Food In Route:

Dolly's Place
511 E Vine St
Vienna, IL 62995
(618) 658-9006
Family style dining

The Chocolate Factory
990 State Hwy 146W
Golconda, IL 62938
877-949-3829, 618-949-3829
Across from Dixon Springs
State Park, 25.7 miles from
Elizabethtown. Chocolates
and ice cream.

RESOURCES

Vienna Chamber of Commerce
618-658-2063

Southern-Most Tourism
800-248-4373

Southwestern Illinois Tourism
800-442-1488

SPECIAL INTEREST

Tunnel Hill State Trail
State Hwy 146 E
Vienna, IL 62995
217-782-9175, 618-658-2168
In the same location as the
Vienna State Park.

Continue west on SR 146. The route leaves Vienna on the busy main road but heads toward a smooth roadway with little traffic. A little later, the road hosts numerous gravel trucks bound for a nearby gravel pit. At 5.8 miles, make a right on SR 37. At 13.4 miles you'll pass Ferne Clyffe State Park. At 14.7 miles you join the AC Route at Goreville. Once past Ferne Clyffe State Park (yesterday's camping option) there is a short bike path that parallels the road. Highlight of the day is the next 20 miles, a relatively flat romp through the Crab Orchard National Wildlife Refuge, where more than 200 species of birds are said to reside.

PLACES TO STAY

Holiday Inn
2300 Reed Station Parkway
Carbondale, IL 62901
800-315-2621, 618-549-2600
$$ ✕ ≈ ▣
Slated to re-open, call first.

Super 8 Motel
1180 E Main Street
Carbondale, IL 62901
800-536-0719, 618-457-8822
$$ ☕

CAMPING

Devil's Kitchen Camp Ground
Devil's Kitchen Lake
Crab Orchard National Wildlife Refuge
1625 Tacoma Lake Road
Carbondale, IL 62901
618-457-5004

Giant City State Park
235 Giant City Road
Makanda, IL 62958
618-457-4836
Recommended by local bike shops.

FOOD & DINING

Hunan Village
710 E Main Street
Carbondale, IL 62901
618-529-1108
Best Asian fusion cuisine on route.

Thai Taste of Carbondale
100 Illinois 13
Carbondale, IL 62901
618-457-6900
Recommended.

SPECIAL INTEREST

Crab Orchard National Wildlife Refuge
8588 Route 148
Marion, IL 62959
618-997-3344 x 334
44,000 acres of parkland.

Southern Illinois University
Carbondale, IL
618-453-2121
Excellent internet access.

RESOURCES

Carbondale Tourism Bureau
815 S Illinois Ave
Carbondale, IL 62901
800-526-1500

Williamson Co. Tourism
1602 Sioux Drive
Marion, IL 62959
800-433-7399, 618-997-3690

Phoenix Cycles
300 S Illinois Avenue
Carbondale, IL 62901
618-549-3612
www.phoenixcycles.net

Carbondale Cycle Shop
303 S Illinois Avenue
Carbondale, IL 62901
618-549-6863

Bike Surgeon
404 S Illinois Avenue
Carbondale, IL 62901
618-457-4521

The old gang at the Carbondale Cycle Shop.

DAY 25 CARBONDALE TO CHESTER, IL
Pop: 8,200   Mileage: 47
Est. Elevation: 1,200
AC Map: 10:115 & 9:114, 113

You'll leave town on the main route and follow the highway, which sports a wide shoulder. At Murphysboro you can either opt for Adventure Cycling's main route, which covers rolling farm lands and hilly backroads, or you can take the Mississippi Levee alternate along the river. Check to make sure that the Mississippi River isn't flooding before you start. It wasn't when we were there.

PLACES TO STAY

Best Western Reid's Inn
2150 State Street
Chester, IL 62233
618-826-3034
$$ ◻ ◿ ▨

Stone House B&B
509 W Harrison Street
Chester, IL 62233
618-826-5465

CAMPING

Cole Memorial Park
Chester, IL 62233
South end of Chester on Hwy 3.

Randolph State and Wildlife Camp Ground
4301 S Lake Drive
Chester, IL 62233
618-826-2706
4.5 miles out of town.

FOOD & DINING

Reid's Harvest House
2440 State Street
Route 150
Chester, IL 62233
618-826-4933
35-foot-long buffet.

McDonalds
2208 State Street
Chester, IL 62233
618-826-2895

Wal-Mart
2206 Illinois /Route 150
Chester, IL 62233
618-826-5041

SPECIAL INTEREST

Popeye Museum
1001 State Street
Chester, IL 62233
618-826-4567

Fort Kaskaskia State Park
4372 Park Rd
Ellis Grove, IL 62241
618-859-3741
At Shawneetown Trail intersection
Camping also available.

RESOURCES

Chester Chamber of Commerce
214 Opdyke Street
Chester, IL 62233
618-826-2721

Randolph County Tourism
1 Taylor Street
Chester, IL 62233
618-826-5000 x 221
www.illinoissouthwest.org

Amish Country

MISSOURI
6 Days - 303.5 Miles

Known for its 55,000 miles of rivers, Missouri tells the story of westward expansion. You'll see and feel that story as you ride through the Ozarks and bump into the Lewis and Clark Trail on your way through this beautiful state. The route takes you through the southern part of the state, missing the more famous big cities but delivering miles of gorgeous countryside. The state's nickname is the "Show Me State," but my husband renamed it the "Show Me the Air Conditioner State" since both the temperatures and the humidity were in the 90s. We beat the heat by starting and ending each day early.

MISSOURI FACTS & RESOURCES

Fast Facts
Population: 5.4 million
Capital: Jefferson City
Nickname: Show Me State
Flower: Hawthorn
Bird: Common Bluebird
Tree: Flowering Dogwood

Key Dates in History
1764   French trading established
1804   Lewis & Clark Expedition departs
1820   Missouri admitted to Union as a slave state
1860   Pony Express begins
1904   World's Fair St. Louis

Missouri Division of Tourism
301 W High St, #290
Jefferson City, MO 65102
800-877-1234
573-751-4133
www.VisitMO.com
tourism@ded.state.mo.us

Missouri Division of Parks
PO Box 176
Jefferson City, MO 65102
800-334-6946
www.mostateparks.org

It's downhill to the Mississippi River to cross the Chester Bridge. Use extreme caution on the bridge as there is no shoulder. The first 10 miles are deliriously flat. Then you'll start to enter the Ozarks, miles and miles of roller coaster roads. The first water stop is at the Sacred Heart Church in Ozora at 21 miles. There are no food stops along the route; so plan on carrying extra supplies and plenty of water, especially if the humidity and temperatures rise. The route goes by two of Missouri's five largest antique stores. St. Mary's Gaint Antique Mall makes an entertaining stop outside of town at 36 miles.

Check Adventure Cycling's web page for route changes between Pilot Knob and Farmington. Also check maps for new routing west of Farmington to Graniteville.

PLACES TO STAY

Tradition Inn
1625 W Columbia Street
(Hwy 97 & Columbia)
Farmington, MO 63640
573-756-8031, 877-355-6205
E-mail:*tradinn@socket.com*
$$ 🚲 🍴 ⛺ 🔲

Days Inn Farmington
1400 Liberty & Hwy 67
Farmington, MO 63640
573-756-8951, 800-329-7466
$$ 🚲 ⛺

Super 8 Motel
930 Valley Creek Rd
(Hwy 67 & Hwy 32)
Farmington, MO 63640
573-756-0344, 800-536-0719
$$ 🚲 ⛺ 🔲

CAMPING

Wilson Rozier City Park
Perrine Road
Farmington, MO 63640
573-756-6686, 573-756-2215
Toilets & water. Call Farmington police or parks first.

Civic Center
Showers available (no camping)
2 Black Knight Drive
Farmington, MO 63640
573-756-0900

Spokes Pub & Grill
Next to the Tradition Inn
1627 W Columbia Street
(Hwy 67 & Columbia)
Farmington, MO 63640
573-756-6220
Decorated in honor of cyclists.

Applebee's
748 Karsch Blvd
Farmington, MO 63640
573-760-0900

SPECIAL INTEREST

St. Mary's Antique Mall
777 7th Street
St. Mary, MO 63673
573-543-2800
Open 7 days a week,
SE Missouri's largest
antique mall.

RESOURCES

**Farmington Chamber
of Commerce**
100 W Broadway Ave
Farmington, MO 63640
800-439-2788, 505-325-0274
www.gofarmington.org

The ride starts out flat for the first 13 miles and then slides into easy rolling hills. Stop by the Fort Davidson Restaurant and Motel at Pilot Knob for breakfast. You'll bike through beautiful Arcadia Valley, known for its iron ore, granite quarries and civil war sites. Many cyclists stop at the Johnson's Shut-Ins State Park, which has a small store, fresh coffee and camping. We went another 10 miles to Lesterville, where water sports thrive on the East Fork of the Black River near its confluence with the West Fork.

PLACES TO STAY

Black River Family Restaurant & Motel
Hwy 21
Lesterville, MO 63654
573-637-2600
$$ ⬦
Has 6 rooms above the restaurant. Dinner weekends only.

Log Cabin Inn Suites
Hwy 21
Lesterville, MO 63654
573-637-2667
$$ ⬦ ▣

Wilderness Lodge & Dining
On Peola Road off Hwy 21 in town
Lesterville, MO 63654
573-637-2295
$$ ⬦ ⚲
Includes breakfast and dinner. Two-night minimum on weekends.

CAMPING

Johnson's Shut-Ins State Park
Route 1
Middlebrook, MO 63656
573-546-2450. Call ahead. Major flooding caused this campground to close temporarily in 2006.

8,670 acres of nature's waterpark. The swift waters of the East Fork of the Black River flow through a canyon-like gorge called a "shut-in." Small store, many recreational activities, trails. 10 miles before Lesterville.

CAMPING

Park's Bluff Campground
199 Elm Street
Lesterville, MO 63654
573-637-2290
Off Hwy 21 in town.

Twin Rivers Landing Camping
Hwy 21
Lesterville, MO 63654
573-637-2274
Across from Log Cabin Inn.

FOOD & DINING

Food In Route:

Fort Davidson Restaurant
302 McClure Street
(Hwy 21 & V)
Pilot Knob, MO 63663
573-546-2719
Open 7 days a week.

Lenny's
31996 Missouri / Hwy 21
Lesterville, MO 63654
573-637-2506
Across from the Log Cabin Inn.
Small grocery, huge liquor store.

SPECIAL INTEREST

Fort Davidson State Historic Site
Hwy 21 & V
Pilot Knob, MO 63663
573-546-3454
Site of Civil War battle.
www.mostateparks.com\
ftdavidson.htm

RESOURCES

Missouri Department of Natural Resources
800-334-6946
www.mostateparks.com

Today's ride starts out relatively flat, at least to the 21 Stop Cafe. At that point the hills will start to remind you of the steep grades in Appalachia. This is the toughest climbing day in the Ozarks. A stop in Ellington, 27 miles from Eminence, is the last Gatorade and food stop on the route. There's also a nice stop at the Owl Bend State Park for a refill. Hydrate, hydrate, hydrate. We drank 462 ounces of liquid on this sweaty day!

Eminence is Missouri's top outpost, according to *Outdoor Life Magazine*. There are more canoes than residents. It's "Where the hills and the rivers meet," on the Ozark National Scenic Riverways; so plan to rent an inner-tube or canoe and ride the river.

PLACES TO STAY

River's Edge Resort
501 N Main Street
Hwy 19 at Jack's Fork Bridge
Eminence, MO 65466
573-226-3233
www.rivers-edge.com
$$$

Shady Lane Cabins & Motel
509 N Main Ave
N Hwy 19
Eminence, MO 65466
573-226-3893
$
One block N of bridge.

Old Blue House B&B
109 S Main Street
Eminence, MO 65466
800-474-9695, 573-226-3498
$$🍵

CAMPING

Jack's Fork Canoe Rental and Campground
Hwy 106
Eminence, MO 65466
800-522-5736, 573-858-3224
East of Eminence.

Harvey's Circle B Campground
Hwy 106 E
Eminence, MO 65466
573-226-3618

**Eminence Canoe
Cottages & Camp**
Missouri 19
Emincence, MO 65466
573-226-3500
West end of town on Jack's Fork.

Ozark Orchard Restaurant
118 N Main Street
Eminence, MO 65466
573-226-3604
Dining on the porch.

Ruby's T & T Restaurant
408 S Main Street
Eminence, MO 65466
573-226-3878
Salad bar.

Captain Jack's Coffee Shop
1/2 mile N of 106 on 19 has wifi
573-226-3942

Windy's Canoes & Tubs
513 N Main Street
Eminence, MO 65466
www.windycanoe.com
573-226-3404
Between Jack's Fork & Hwy 106
Junction

Alley Spring Grist Mill
Hwy 106
573-226-3318
Eminence, MO 65466
6 miles out of town.

**Eminence Chamber of
Commerce**
PO Box 415
Eminence, MO 65466
573-226-3318

Ozark National Scenic Riverways
National Park Headquarters
573-323-4236
www.nps.gov

You're officially in the Ozark Scenic Riverways today with many more ups and downs. The second half of the day takes you to pastures and nicely rolling grades, a welcome respite from all those hills. The ride ends in a classic American town with its old courthouse, library and post office, marred slightly by a highway lined with fast food joints and strip malls. The Houston public library has internet access.

PLACES TO STAY

Southern Inn Motel
1493 S Sam Houston Blvd
Houston, MO 65483
417-967-4591
$ ☕

Lazy L Motel
1121 S Sam Houston Blvd,
Hwy 63
Houston, MO 65483
417-967-4117
$ 回

CAMPING

Emmett Kelly City Park
Houston, MO 65483
417-967-3348
Toilets, no shower.

West Side Park
Quiter than Emmett Kelly Park
Call sheriff: 417-967-4165

FOOD & DINING

Numerous fast food joints and pizza parlors.

SPECIAL INTEREST

A major revitalization effort with the help of the state of Missouri started to preserve the old town in 2000.

Forbes Pharmacy
100 N Grand Avenue
Houston, MO 65483
Open for 137 years.

Houston Area Chamber of Commerce
501 E Walnut
Houston, MO 65483
417-967-2220
www.houstonchamber.com

Houston Parks & Recreation
601 S Grand Avenue
Houston, MO 65483
417-967-3348

Texas County Library
117 W Walnut
Houston, MO 65483
417-967-2258
Internet access.

Alternate transportation in Missouri

Surprise. There's still more hill-climbing on this 65-mile-long day. You'll roll through farmlands filled with cows, horses, goats and carpets of pink daisies. What looks like a closed, run-down grocery store with old filling station gas pumps may turn out to be a thriving business. (Look for Cobbles Corner and the Missouri cousins.) The quaint town of Marshfield is long gone to I-44 and its fast food chains. Watch for lots of traffic as you ride into town on a busy two-lane road.

PLACES TO STAY

Dickey House B&B
331 S Clay Street
Marshfield, MO 65706
417-468-3000
www.dickeyhouse.com
$$$ ▽

Holiday Inn Express
1301 Banning Street
Marshfield, MO 65706
417-859-6000, 800-315-2621
$$ ▣

The Plaza Hotel
113 State Hwy W
Marshfield, MO 65706
417-859-2491
$

CAMPING

Marshfield City Park
North Marshfield
Marshfield, MO 65706
417-468-2310.
Call city hall first. All amenities and pool.

FOOD & DINING

Numerous

SPECIAL INTEREST

Walnut Spring Farm & Museum
1414 Old Wire Road
Marshfield, MO 65706
417-859-7954

RESOURCES

Marshfield Chamber of Commerce
1350 Spur Drive, #190
Marshfield, MO 65706
417-859-3925

This is your last full day of Ozark hills but another grand day of cycling. We discovered a back route to Everton which bypasses Ash Grove completely. At Walnut Grove continue straight on "U" instead of turning left on "V." Go 10 miles on State Rt. 160. Make a left to Everton. It's a straighter, better, and less busy route. Several towns and stops throughout the day provide plenty of food and water.

PLACES TO STAY

Unfortunately the only place to stay in Everton closed.

CAMPING

Running Springs Farm
RR 1 Box 254
Everton, MO 65646
417-535-2190
Call for directions.

FOOD & DINING

At press time the only restaurant had closed but there is a tavern on Main Street.

SPECIAL INTEREST

Tim Hill's Civil War Cannons
Tim's reproduction cannons were used by PBS in a TV documentary on Wilson's Creek Battle.
417-880-6991

RESOURCES

Everton City Hall
116 W Commercial Street
Everton, MO 65646
417-535-6025

Everton Fire Dept.
417-535-2605

Tim Hill's famous cannon

The Ozarks hilly roads. IstockPhoto.com

92 Kansas

KANSAS
9 Days - 531 Miles

Flat, beautiful and hardly boring. That's Kansas in a nutshell. Cyclists often complain about headwinds when they go from west to east. We researched the prevailing winds and found, in fact, that they predominantly come from the south. Also watch for big rain storms. It rained 4.2 inches in two days while we were in Chanute.

KANSAS FACTS & RESOURCES

Fast Facts
Population: 2.6 million
Capital: Topeka
Nickname: The Sunflower State
Flower: Sunflower
Bird: Western Meadowlark
Tree: Cottonwood

Key Dates in History
1804   Lewis & Clark camp on Missouri River
1854   Kansas Territory open
1861   Kansas 34th State
1862   Homestead Act -160 acres for $10

Kansas Division of Tourism
1000 Jackson, Suite 100
Topeka, KS 66603
785-296-2009
800-2KANSAS
www.travelks.com

Road & Weather Information
800-585-7623

DAY 32 EVERTON, MO, TO PITTSBURG, KS
Pop: 17,800
Mileage: 58.5
Est. Elevation: 1,000
AC Map: 9:102,101,100

You'll still be rolling through the last hills of the Ozarks before it flattens out in Kansas. But then, it's finally flat at last. Last stop in Missouri is Golden City, about 27 miles from Everton, where many cyclists stop at Cooky's Cafe and sign the guest book. There are no food or water stops between Golden City and Pittsburg, but the road is so completely flat that if you're lucky and pick up a tail wind, you'll just fly into Pittsburg. Three miles from town is the Bison Red Deer Wildlife Preserve, available for viewing.

PLACES TO STAY

Holiday Inn Express
Hwy 69, 4011 Parkview Drive
Pittsburg, KS 66762
620-231-8700
$$ 🚮🏊◎

Super 8 Motel
3108 N Broadway
Pittsburg, KS 66762
620-232-1881, 800-536-0719
$$ 🚮🏊

Comfort Inn
4009 Parkview Drive
Pittsburg, KS 66762
620-231-8800, 888-300-8800
$$🏊◎

CAMPING

Kansas Association of RV Parks and Campground
877-526-2782
www.ksrvparks.com
Additional resource for camping throughout the state.

Pittsburg RV Park
20th & Route 69
620-231-4100
Pittsburg, KS 66762

Lincoln City Park & Pool
Pittsburg, KS 66762
620-231-8310

Bison Mined Land Wildlife Preserve
Pittsburg, KS 66762
620-231-3173
Three miles north of Pittsburg on Hwy 69.

FOOD & DINING

Food In Route:
Cooky's Cafe
519 Main Street
Golden City, MO 64748
417-537-4741
Sign the biker's journal. Closed on Monday. Great blueberry pancakes and lemon chiffon pie.

El Charro Mexican Restaurant
3102 N Broadway
Pittsburg, KS 66762
620-232-5763
Beer and Margaritas.

Western Sizzlin' Steakhouse
2711 N Broadway
Pittsburg, KS 66762
620-232-1007
Across from Wal-Mart
Large salad bar.

SPECIAL INTEREST

Bicycle Adventures
109 E Rose
Pittsburg, KS 66762
620-231-7727
Bike shop closed Sunday.

Pedal Power
115 E 6th Street
Pittsburg, KS 66762
620-230-0650
Bike shop - limited hours.

Tailwind Cyclists
1511 N Broadway
Pittsburg, KS 66762
620-231-2212
Closed Sunday. On route to motels.

Antiques in Pittsburg
Pittsburg is a Mecca for antiques, large and small. Check the directory at the Visitor's Bureau.

RESOURCES

Crawford County Convention & Visitors Bureau
117 W 4th Street
Pittsburg, KS 66762
620-231-1212, 800-879-1112
www.visitcrawfordcounty.com

Pittsburg State University
1701 S Broadway Street
Pittsburg, KS 66762
620-231-7000
Large bank of computers for internet access.

Pittsburg Chamber of Commerce
117 W 4th Street
Pittsburg, KS 66762
620-231-1212

Chanute is "the Hub of Southeast Kansas" on the Neosho River. You'll find your first espresso in the almost 300 miles since Eminence. It's almost a flat run to Chanute through soy, corn and oil fields. Look for the Kansas Historical Marker at around 47 miles – the site of the first Indian School in Kansas at the town of Shaw. In 1865 the Indians were removed to Oklahoma as part of a treaty. Chanute is an old railroad town with a great tourism center located in the restored station.

PLACES TO STAY

Super 8 Motel
3502 S Santa Fe
Chanute, KS 66720
620-431-7788, 800-536-0719
$$ ▯

Guest House Motor Inn
1814 S Santa Fe -35th Street
Chanute, KS 66720
620-431-0600, 800-523-6128
$ ≋

CAMPING

Sante Fe Safari Camp Ground
Santa Fe Ave & Canute 35 Pkwy
Chanute, KS 66720
620-431-5250
www.chanute.org

Yodling Katy's
.4 miles north of junction off Santa Fe (US 169). Free camping on Katy's property.
Call: 620-431-4038.

FOOD & DINING

Many good places and local hangouts.

SPECIAL INTEREST

Downtown Chanute
Make sure that you get downtown to see the Visitor Center, housed in the 1903 Santa Fe Train Depot, once home to the Santa Fe Railroad and one of Kansas's largest train stations. The town benefited from oil and gas money in the early 1900s. Numerous stately buildings still remain. Flea market shops abound.

Self-Guided Walking Tour
Directory of Landmark Buildings
available at the Visitor's Center.

Chanute Art Gallery
17 N Lincoln
Chanute, KS 66720
620-431-7807

**Martin & Osa Johnson Safari
Museum**
111 N Lincoln
Chanute, KS 66720
620-431-2730

Chanute Visitor's Center
E Elm Street
Chanute, KS 66720
620-431-5229
Email: information@
chanutechamber.com
www.chanutechamber.com

Chanute Chamber
21 N Lincoln Avenue
Chanute, KS 66720
620-431-3350, 877-431-3350
www.chanutechamber.com

Chanute town park.

Today's ride is mostly flat with a rare Kansas-style hill. The route passes beautiful green pastures and yellow wheat fields. There are several spots for Gatorade refills. You'll bike past Toronto Lake, which boasts 194 bird types. A nearby ghost town was once settled by the Canadians. A little further down the road at about 43 miles is the famous Lizard Lips Cafe, where you can pick up a little plastic lizard as a souvenir of your Kansas sojourn.

PLACES TO STAY

Blue Stem Lodge
1314 E River Street
Eureka, KS 67045
620-583-5531
$$▱⌣

Carriage House Motel
201 S Main Street
Eureka, KS 67045
620-583-5501
$

CAMPING

Eureka City Park
Main Street
Eureka, KS 67045
Call police to register.
620-583-4640
Swimming pool.

FOOD & DINING

Food In Route:
Lizard Lips Grill & Deli
153 Hwy 54
Toronto, KS 66777
620-637-2384
Great pies, plastic lizards.
11 miles west of Yates Center.

SPECIAL INTEREST

Eureka Downs
"Horse Racing Capital of Kansas."

Toronto-Fall River State Parks
144 Hwy 105
Toronto, KS 66777
620-637-2213
"Bird watching is the most
popular outdoor activity in
Kansas."

RESOURCES

Chamber of Commerce
309 N Oak Street
Eureka, KS 67045
620-583-5452

The latest thing in TransAm wheels

Flat roads continue throughout the day with a lovely shoulder on Hwy 54. You'll pass a wild mustang horse ranch, hundreds of cattle farms and travel through the famous Blue Stem pastures of the Flint Hills. Newton is the home of the Turkey Red Grain Wheat brought to Kansas by the Mennonites. This is also the site of the Kansas Chisholm Trail where Longhorn cattle drives from Texas once terminated and the cattle transported by railroad north. At one point a herd of 50 Black Angus followed us on our bikes. Bikers - a new breed of cattle rustlers? At approximately 34 miles you make a left on 150th Street. From there it's 40 unbelievably straight miles to Newton.

PLACES TO STAY

Best Western Red Coach Inn
1301 E First Street
Newton, KS 67114
316-283-9120, 800-780-7234
$$⛵🏊

Days Inn Newton
105 Manchester Avenue
Newton, KS 67114
316-283-3330
$$🏊

Econo Lodge
1620 E Second
Newton, KS 67114
316-283-7611
$

CAMPING

City Athletic Park
Free camping, pool.
316-284-6083

Walton's Recreation Park
6 miles E of Newton.
316-283-8350

FOOD & DINING

Reba's Restaurant
301 N Main Street
Newton, KS 67114
316-283-9800

Food In Route:
Old Hat Café
578 SE Rosalia Rd
Rosalia, KS 67132
620-476-2240
Sign the biker's book.
Good spot for breakfast.

Kauffman Museum
Bethel College
2801 N Main Street
Newton, KS 67117
316-283-1612
Prairie life and Mennonite story.

Country Boys Carriage
1504 S Rock Road
Newton, KS 67114
316-283-2636

Bethel College
300 27th Street
Newton, KS 67117
316-283-2500
Oldest Mennonite liberal arts
college in North America.

RESOURCES

**Newton Chamber of Commerce
and Visitor Bureau**
500 N Main Street, Suite 101
Newton, KS 67114
316-283-2560

The "Flint Hills" of Kansas

Today offers another beautiful ride through sunflowers, more Red Turkey Wheat and soy bean fields on flat, flat roads. Check out Daylite Donuts down the road from Newton. You'll like Sterling 3 miles off route and well worth the detour. This little town gets a gold star for effort. Sterling has been restored with Federal "Main Street" funds, giving it gentle sidewalks, old-fashioned underground lamps, and restored historic buildings. It also has a great campground.

PLACES TO STAY

Country Inn
430 S Broadway, Sterling, KS 67579
620-904-4424
$

Prairie Garden B&B
320 E Monroe, Sterling, KS 67579
620-204-6500
$$

Sterling Chamber of Commerce
(Check here for places to stay)
112 S Broadway
Sterling, KS 67579
620-278-2099

CAMPING

Lake Sterling Park & Campground
Sterling, KS 67579
620-278-3423
Pool, off main street.

FOOD & DINING

Food in Route:
Daylite Donuts.
349 N Old 81 Hwy
Hestor, KS 67062
620-327-4888
Breakfast donuts 6 miles from Newton. Makes Krispy Kreme cry.

Back Porch Grill
317 S Broadway
Sterling, KS 67579
620-278-3069

Paddy's Restaurant
313 S Broadway Ave
Sterling, KS 67579
620-278-3276
Next door to the Grill.
The local hangout.

Gambinos Pizza
102 N Broadway Ave
Sterling, KS 67579
620-278-3400
Kansas-style pizza.

This is another flat but delight-fully scenic ride. You'll enjoy farms and pastures and the lovely rolling hills of Kansas again today, but there are no services along the route; so take plenty of food and water. Stop at the Quivira National Wildlife Refuge for bird- watching. Larned, namesake of Fort Larned on the Santa Fe Trail, is a cattle and wheat town, with plenty of feed lots to fatten up the delicous local steaks.

PLACES TO STAY

Best Western Townsman Inn
123 E 14th Street
Larned, KS 67550
620-285-3114, 800-780-7234
$$ 🚲♨️🖥️

Country Inn Motel
135 E 14th Street
Larned, KS 67550
620-285-3216
$

CAMPING

Schnack Lowrey Park
Carroll Avenue
Call police: 620-285-8505
Pool.

Larned Village Campground
US 156
Larned, KS 67550
316-285-3261
Private campground.

FOOD & DINING

Scraps Coffee Shop
612 Broadway Street
Larned, KS 67550
620-285-8977
Best hospitality on entire route!

Quivira National Wildlife Refuge
Rural Route 3
Stafford, KS 67578
800-344-WILD, 620-486-2393
www.fws.gov
Over 300 species of migratory
birds have been observed in this
refuge.

The Santa Fe Trail Center
Historical Museum & Library
1349 K185 Hwy
Larned, KS 67550
Route 3, 2 miles west of Larned
620-285-2054
www.awav.net/trailctr/
Closed Mondays. Begun in 1821,
the trail was a two-way freight
route between the US and Mexico
for trade. It once stretched more
than 900 miles from central
Missouri through Kansas to SE
Colorado and into NE New
Mexico.

Winter Wheat Harvest
During the wheat season watch
out for the caravans of "Custom
Harvesters" making their way up
from Texas, following the ripening
crops and temporarily hogging the
road. Pull over and let them pass.
They're a lot bigger than you!

RESOURCES

Kansas Wheat Commission
1990 Kimball Ave
Manhatten, KS 66502
785-539-0255
www.kswheat.com

DAY 38 LARNED TO NESS CITY, KS
Pop: 1,700
Mileage: 65
Est. Elevation: 1,000
AC Map: 8:89, 88, 87 & 7:86

The first 19 miles of the day run due north; so, if you have a typical southern tail wind, you'll fly. There's a new rest area 45 miles from Larned with restrooms and cold water. It's another day of mostly flat and very straight roads. At Rush Center you make a left on SR 96 and will virtually stay on SR 96 all the way to Colorado. If you're traveling during wheat harvest, you'll stay entertained by counting the caravans of "Custom Harvesters" that zoom by you.

PLACES TO STAY

Derrick Inn Motel
409 E Sycamore, Hwy 96
Ness City, KS 67560
785-798-3617
$ ⊽ ✕

Wagon Wheel B&B
Ness City, KS 67560
www.wagonwheelonline.com

CAMPING

City Pool & Park
Lake Street
Ness City, KS 67560
Call police: 785-798-3611

FOOD & DINING

Cactus Club Restaurant
124 S Pennsylvania Ave
795-798-3639
Ness City, KS 67560

SPECIAL INTEREST

Ness County Bank Building
102 W Main at Pennsylvania
Ness City, KS 67560
785-798-3337
"Skyscraper of the plains."
.Four-story limestone building.
Built in 1890. Sells Kansas-made items in gift shop.

RESOURCES

102 W Main Street
Ness City, KS 67560
785-798-2413

Sixteen miles down the road from Ness City is a historical marker, the "Homestead of a Genius, George Washington Carver," born in 1864. The route is straight all the way to Scott City. There's only one coffee stop, at 31 miles in the town of Dighton. Look for fresh donuts. Commercial cattle feeding is the number one industry in Scott County, which claims more than 60 commercial and private feedlots.

PLACES TO STAY

Chaparral Inn Motel
102 Main Street
Scott City, KS 67871
620-872-2181
$

Cowboy Kevin's
Hwy 96, 503 E Fifth
Scott City, KS 67871
620-872-8993
$

Airliner Motel
Hwy 96, 609 E Fifth St
Scott City, KS 67871
620-872-2125
$

The Guest House B&B
311 E Fifth
Scott City, KS 67871
620-872-3559
$$

Athletic Club Hostel
104 S Washington Street
Scott City, KS 67871
Showers, pool, sleep on gym floor
620-872-3807

CAMPING

City Park
Main Street & 2nd
Scott City, KS 67871
Sheriff's office: 620-397-2452

Palmer Park
Pool.

RESOURCES

Scott City Chamber of Commerce
113 E Fifth Street
Scott City, KS 67871
620-872-3525

The road continues as straight as an arrow. It has a shoulder all the way to Leoti, 25 miles away, where you'll find the one coffee stop in the day. There's one motel in Tribune, right across from the truck stop and appropriately named "Trails End." The friendly Tribune library has internet access.

PLACES TO STAY

Trails End Motel
110 W Kansas Avenue
Tribune, KS 67879
620-376-4236
$

CAMPING

Tribune City Park
Zenaide Street
Tribune, KS 67879
Call police before camping:
620-376-4543
Pool.

FOOD & DINING

Elliott's GastroPub
314 W Kansas Ave
Tribune, KS 67879
620-376-2277

SPECIAL INTEREST

Horace Greeley Museum
214 East Harper
Tribune, KS 67879
620-376-4996
Built in 1890 out of native sandstone, the museum is on the National Register of Historic Places. Horace Greeley founded and edited the New York Tribune.

Greeley County Chamber
510 Broadway
Tribune, KS 67879
620-376-2548

Horace Greeley Museum

COLORADO
9 Days - 431 Miles

The highest state in the Union with an average elevation of 6,800 feet will take your breath away as you make multiple crossings of the Continental Divide. Sometimes called "the Rooftop of America," its official nickname, the Centennial State, comes from its entry into the Union 100 years after the signing of the Declaration of Independence.

COLORADO FACTS & RESOURCES

Fast Facts
Population: 3.9 million
Capital: Denver
Nickname: Centennial or Silver State
Flower: Rocky Mountain Columbine
Bird: Lark Bunting
Tree: Colorado Blue Spruce

Key Dates in History
1500s   Spaniards in Colorado
1803   Louisiana Purchase acquires Colorado
1804   First American exploration
1858   Colorado Gold Rush
1876   Colorado 38th state

Colorado Travel & Tourism Authority
1625 Broadway
Suite 2700
Denver, CO 80202
800-265-6723, 303-892-3840
www.colorado.com

It's a totally straight stretch of road again today with one coffee stop 32 miles down the road at a real gas station. The flat lands, bluestem pastures and wheat fields of Kansas slowly merge into lush green sagebrush and wide open, short-grass plains. You cross into Colorado at about 16 miles. At 42 miles you'll pass the site of the Sandy Creek Massacre where 150 peaceful Cheyenne and Arapaho women and children were killed in 1884, thus ending an era of peace on the plains. A signpost at the crossroads of Hwys 287 and 96 sums up Eads: "Agriculture and recreation combine in a town where family and community still come first."

PLACES TO STAY

The Econo Lodge
609 E 15th Street South
Hwy 96
Eads, CO 81036
719-438-5451
$

CAMPING

City Park
Maine Street
Eads, CO 81036
Library & services across street.

FOOD & DINING

Michael's Truck Stop
901 Wansted St
Eads, CO 81036
719-438-5639

K&M Ranch House
505 W 15th St
Eads, CO 81036
719-438-2002

SPECIAL INTEREST

Sandy Creek Massacre Site
Famous site on the Big Sandy Creek thought by some to have triggered the Great Indian Wars.

**The Great Buffalo Hunt
Historical Marker – 1872**
Thirty million buffalo roamed
these plains in the early 19th
century. "Twenty-one year old
Grand Duke Alexis of Russia
while visiting Denver was
promised a buffalo hunt. The
escort included: Gen. Philip
Sheridan, Lt. Col. George
Custer, Buffalo Bill Cody, Wild
Bill Hickock, Kit Carson held
at Sandy Creek. The success of
the gala hunt, along with the
large amounts of champagne and
whiskey, greatly improved the
relations between Russia and the
US."

Nails By Marni
1315 Maine
Eads, CO 81036
719-438-5862
OK, so I may be the only cyclist
to get a manicure in the middle
of nowhere on a 4,000-mile bike
trip, but, hey, why not?

RESOURCES

Eads Chamber of Commerce
110 W 13th Street
Eads, CO 81036
719-438-5590
www.plainsonline.net
www.plainsnetwork.com

Kiowa Press
1208 Maine Street
Eads, CO 81036
719-438-5800
www.kiowacountypress.com

Colorado Welcome Committee Chair

Another straight shot of high-plains cycling with a surprise coffee stop at Haswell about 23 miles down the road. Haswell boasts the "Nation's Smallest Jail," built in 1921. The gas station supplies the necessary coffee and Gatorade. Next stop is Sugar City just 5 miles outside of Ordway.

Ordway KOA & JR's Country Store
18055 Country Road G
SR 96 & SR 71
Ordway, CO
719-267-3262
Private campground, grocery and restaurant.

PLACES TO STAY

Hotel Ordway
132 Colorado Avenue
Ordway, CO 81063
719-267-3541
$
Owned by Madeline Ferguson, the hotel's former maid.

CAMPING

Hotel Ordway
Reasonably priced and welcoming for cyclists.
719-267-3541

Ordway City Park
Ordway, CO 81063

FOOD & DINING

Food In Route:
Sugar City Cafe
Colorado St & E Adams Ave
Sugar City, CO 81076
Open for breakfast. Closed Friday and Saturday. 5 miles outside of Ordway.

In Ordway:
Beans To Go
126 Colorado Avenue
Ordway, CO 81063
719-267-3476
Next to hotel. Stuffed sopapillas, homemade by Ordway Hotel owner's son Tom Campos and nephew.

Saucer Block Restaurant
Out of business.

Bits and Spurs Café
212 Main Street
Ordway, CO 81063
719-267-3996
Home cookin'.

RESOURCES

Ordway Chamber of Commerce
PO Box 133
Ordway, CO 81063
Town Hall: 719-267-3134
City: 719-267-4741

You'll get your first glimpse of the Rockies at 11 miles in Olney Springs. Most of the day you'll parallel the Arkansas River. At about 30 miles you'll come to the Boone Grocery & Hardware Store which opens at 8 a.m. for chimichangas and coffee. About 15 miles before Pueblo you'll be grateful for the big shoulder on Hwy 50. Hundreds of prairie dogs await by the roadside to give you a standing ovation as you enter town. Pueblo is a good place to get your bikes tuned up for the mountains ahead and to take a stopover day.

PLACES TO STAY

Abriendo Inn
300 W Abriendo Avenue
Pueblo, CO 81004
719-544-6544
$$$ ▷
National Register of Historic Places.

Santa Fe Inn
730 N Santa Fe Ave
Pueblo, CO 81004
719-543-6530
$$ ▷

Hampton Inn
4790 Eagleridge Circle
Pueblo, CO 81004
719-543-6500
$$ ▷

Super 8
1100 W US Hwy 50
Pueblo, CO 81004
719-545-4104
$

CAMPING

Lake Pueblo State Park
719-561-9320

KOA Pueblo Kampground
9040 Interstate 25
Pueblo, CO 81004
716-676-3376

FOOD & DINING

Food In Route:
Boone Grocery & Hardware
410 Main Street
Boone, CO 81025
719-947-0559
30 miles to the first coffee stop
from Ordway. Opens at 8 a.m.
Super chimichangas. Closed on
Sunday.

Lots of food choices.

SPECIAL INTEREST

Historic Riverwalk
Opened in 2000, the Riverwalk is
a 26-acre urban waterfront.

Union Avenue Historic District
Pueblo Historic Society
201 W "B" Street
Pueblo, CO 81004
719-543-6772
Once a steel town, this restored
historic district offers walking
tours and plenty of restaurants
and shops.

RESOURCES

Great Divide Bike Store
400 N Santa Fe Avenue
Pueblo, CO 81003
719-546-2453

Bob's Bicycle
2625 N Elizabeth Street
Pueblo, CO 81003
719-543-8373

Vance's Bicycle World
2200 S Prairie Ave
Pueblo, CO 81005
719-566-6925
Very knowledgeable.

**Greater Pueblo Chamber of
Commerce**
302 N Santa Fe Avenue
Pueblo, CO 81003
800-233-3446, 719-542-1776
www.pueblochamber.org

B&B Innkeepers of Colorado
800-265-7696
www.innsofcolorado.org

Historic Riverwalk in Pueblo, CO

DAY 44 PUEBLO TO CANON CITY, CO
Pop: 12,700
Mileage: 46
Est. Elevation: 1,200
AC Map: 6:73, 72

Leaving Pueblo, there's a wide shoulder on Hwy 50 for easy, comfortable riding. Today you'll ride through huge ranches in the foothills of the Rockies. Watch for very heavy traffic in Canon City. If you have time, jump the train to tour the Royal Gorge in Canon City.

PLACES TO STAY

Best place to stay in town is at the west end in the old historic district across from the Royal Gorge.

Econo Lodge
311 Royal Gorge Blvd
Canon City, CO 81212
719-276-6900
$$ 🛏 ✕

Super 8 Motel
209 N 19th St
Canon City, CO 81212
719-275-8687
$$

America's Best Value Inn
1925 Fremont Drive
Canon City, CO 81212
719-275-3377
$$ 🛏 ✕ 🌊

CAMPING

Maverick Trailer & RV Park
295 S Raynolds Avenue
Canon City, CO 81212
719-275-5546

RV Station Campground
3120 E Main
Canon City, CO 81212
719-275-4576
2.5 miles off route.

Royal Gorge KOA Campground
559 Country Rd 3A
Canon City, CO 81212
719-275-6116
8 miles west of town toward Guffey.

Yogi Bear's Jellystone Campground
Hwy 50 and 9 Junction
719-276-6813
9 miles west of Canon City. Limited stores and services.

Florence City Park
(Along the route)
Allows camping.
Check in with sheriff.
719-784-4848

(Stephanie - can you please choose
a restaurant online in the yellow
pages)

SPECIAL INTEREST

Royal Gorge Railroad
330 Royal Gorge Blvd
Canon City, CO 81212
888-RAILS-4U
717-276-4000,888-724-5748
www.royalgorgeroute.com
24 mile, two-hour train ride
through 1,000-foot-deep gorge.
Travels under world's highest
suspension bridge.

Museum of Colorado Prisons
201 N 1st Street
Canon City, CO 81212
719-269-3015
www.prisonmuseum.org

Dinosaur Depot
330 Royal Gorge Blvd
Canon City, CO 81212
719-269-7150
Next to train station.

RESOURCES

**Canon City Chamber of
Commerce**
403 Royal Gorge Blvd
Canon City, CO 81212
719-275-2331

Red Canon Cycles
410 Main Street
Canon City CO
719-285-8169
www.redcanoncycles.com

View from the Royal Gorge Train

This is a big climbing day, 4,300 feet. You'll be cycling to an elevation of 8,500 in some of the loveliest country on the trip. These are long, gradual climbs, unlike the ones in the Appalachians, which were sometimes painfully steep. It's hard to tell where the road and the sky stop. You'll feel like a high-plains drifter. Guffey, established in 1896, is two miles off route but worth the detour. It's home to the annual Fourth of July Chicken Flying Contest. Held at high noon, the record chicken flight was 138 feet. Guffey is the only city in Colorado with a cat for a mayor. His name is Monster and he resides in the Guffey Garage.

PLACES TO STAY

Peaceful Henry's Rooms
Guffey, CO 80820
719-650-2996
$
Mark Johnson contact.

CAMPING

Bill & Colleen Soux
PO Box 2
Guffey, CO 80820
719-689-3291
Cabin B&B with outhouse and camping available.

FOOD & DINING

Freshwater Saloon & Guffey General Store
52B S 8th Street
Guffey, CO 80820
719-689-0518

SPECIAL INTEREST

Fourth of July Chicken Fly Guffey Garage
PO Box 2
Guffey, CO 80820
719-689-3291

CAMPING: Royal Gorge

Fort George RV Park
7.5 miles W of Cañon City. 1/2
mile before Royal Gorge
45044 US Hwy 50
719-275-5111

KOA
559 County Rd 3A
Canon City, CO 81215
719-276-5-6116
1/2 mile off route towards
Royal Gorge.

Yogi Bear's Jellystone Campground
Hwy 50 and 9 Junction
719-276-6813
9 miles west of Canon City.
Limited stores and services.

This is a day to dream about, a glorious ride through the high meadows and wonderous parklands. Probably the best scenery to date, except for yesterday and tomorrow. Gentle climbs continue. At 11 miles you'll go through Currant Creek Pass at 9,404 feet with views that go on forever. At 29 miles you enter the South Platte River Valley.

Fairplay, at 10,000 feet, started in 1859 when gold was discovered. Every man was going to have a "fairplay" on his claim. Each man's claim was no more than he could work. Fairplay is now a restored Western town with lots of history.

PLACES TO STAY

Hand Hotel B&B
531 Front Street
Fairplay, CO 80440
719-836-3595
www.handhotel.com
$$$✕

Western Inn
490 Hwy 285
Fairplay, CO 80440
719-836-2026
$$
.3 miles N of junction SR 9

CAMPING

There is no camping in the town of Fairplay itself. Call US Forest Service: 719-836-2031.

Western Inn
490 Hwy 285
Fairplay, CO 80440
719-836-2026
Some camping available.

FOOD & DINING

Brown Burro Cream & Steam
702 Main Street
Fairplay, CO 80440
719-836-2335

South Park City
100 4th Street
Fairplay, CO 80440
719-836-2387
www.coloradodirectory.com/
southparkmuseum
A beautifully preserved 19th
century mining town with
32 vintage buildings and 60,000
artifacts.

High Alpine Sports
525 Main Street
Fairplay, CO 80440
719-836-0201

**South Park Chamber of
Commerce**
719-836-3410
www.southparkchamber.com

Highest saloon in the US at 10,000 feet in Fairplay, Colorado

The first five miles is on a lovely, paved bike path between Fairplay and Alma. As the road starts to climb Hoosier Pass on an extremely busy two-lane highway, use caution. Hoosier Pass, at 11,542 feet is the highest point on the TransAm route. It was first crossed by John Fremont in 1844 and named for the men who came from Indiana to work on the "Hoosier Gulch Mine" in 1860. From the top, it's 12 screaming miles downhill with lots of curves into Breckinridge.

PLACES TO STAY

Allaire Timbers Inn
9511 Colorado 9
Breckinridge, CO 80424
970-453-7530, 800-624-4904
$$$$ ☕

Abbett Placer Inn
205 S French Street
Breckinridge, CO 80424
970-453-6489

B&B on North Main Street
303 North Main Street
Breckinridge, CO 80424
800-795-2975, 970-543-2975
$$$ ☕
www.breckinridge-inn.com

CAMPING

Fireside Inn Hostel
114 N French Street
Breckinridge, CO 80424
970-453-6456

Camping further down the road in Frisco.

Heaton Bay Campground
Dillon Reservoir
Bike Path
Frisco, CO
877-444-6777

FOOD & DINING

Endless possibilities.

Daylight Donuts
305 N Main Street
Breckenridge, CO 80424
970-453-2548
Good place for very affordable full breakfast

SPECIAL INTEREST

South Main Street Historic District, Historical Society
403 La Bonte Street
Dillon, CO 80424
970-468-2207

Bike Path
40-mile paved bike path from Breckinridge to Vail.

RESOURCES

Breckinridge Resort Chamber
111 Ski Hill Rd
Breckinridge, CO 80424
970-453-6018, 800-221-1091
www.gobreck.com

Breckinridge B&B Association
www.colorado-bnb.com/breckinns

Avalanche Sports
540 S. Main St.
970-453-1461
Breckinridge, CO 80424

The Mayor of Guffey, Colorado

The first miles from Breckinridge to Frisco are on a paved bike path along the Blue River. Once in Frisco, the going gets a bit more confusing. At 9 miles you exit the bike path, rejoining it at 10 miles to ride along the Dillon Reservoir to Silverthorne. Use caution in Silverthorne and on the way to Kremmling. Just pull off and wait for trucks and SUVs to pass. At 35 miles is the Prairie Point Campground on the White River. At 51 miles you'll cross the Colorado River for the first time as you enter Kremmling.

PLACES TO STAY

Cliffside Inn Hotel
113 N 6th Street
Kremmling, CO 80459
877-CLIFFSIDE, 970-724-9620
$$ 🔲

Bob's Western Motel
110 W Park Avenue, Hwy 40
Kremmling, CO 80459
970-724-3266
$

Hotel Easton
105 S 2nd Street on Hwy 40
Kremmling, CO 80459
800-516-0815, 970-724-3261
$$ ☕

River of Life Log Cabin Lodging
W Park Avenue
Kremmling, CO 80459
970-724-9559
$$ 7 log cabins withkitchenettes. West end of Hwy 40. Check in Cliffside.

CAMPING

Kremmling City Park
Kremmling, CO 80459
Behind the fire station. Restroom at old, not new, fire department.

Hotel Easton
105 S 2nd
Kremmling, CO 80459
800-546-0815, 970-724-3261

Red Mountain RV Park and Campground
1.2 miles east of downtown Kremmling on US 40.
970-724-9593

Wolford Mountain Recreation Area
7 miles beyond Kremmling, 1 mile E on CR 230.
970-531-1353

FOOD & DINING

Quarter Circle Saloon
Main Street
Kremmling, CO 80459
970-724-9601
Homemade Mex and great steaks.

RESOURCES

Kremmling Area Chamber of Commerce
203 Park Avenue
Kremmling, CO 80459
970-724-3472
www.Kremmlingchamber.com

Great Divide Bike Shop in Pueblo, Colorado

Editor's note: Maps show new, better routing on US 40 from Kremmling to SR125 to Walden.

Walden is the "Moose Viewing Capital of Colorado." There were no services for 62 miles from Kremmling to Waldon on the old route. You'll travel through the spectacular North Park region of the Rockies, with elevations to 8,772 feet. At about 27 miles you'll make another crossing of the Continental Divide at Willow Creek Pass and then head downhill to Waldon. You cross the Illinois River on the way into town and the Michigan River on the way out of town.

PLACES TO STAY

Westside Motel
441 Lafever Street
Walden, CO 80480
970-723-8589
$$

Hoover Roundup Motel & RV Park
365 Main Street
Walden, CO 80480
970-723-4680
$$

CAMPING

Granite Corner RV Park
Off LeFevre St near 4th St
Walden, CO 80480
970-723-4628

FOOD & DINING

Moose Creek Restaurant
508 Main Street
Walden, CO 80480
970-723-8272
Was an old Chevron station. Best food in Walden.

Riverock Cafe
460 Main Street
Walden, CO 80480
970-723-4670
Fresh muffins and old books.

SPECIAL INTEREST

Moose Viewing
970-871-2841
The Colorado Division of
Wildlife reintroduced moose into
the North Park region.

North Park Pioneer Museum
87 Logan Street
Walden, CO 80480
970-723-3282
Behind the Jackson County
Courthouse.

Walden
The US Census Bureau defines
a frontier as population density
fewer than two people per square
mile. Walden, which claims to be
the "Last frontier in America," has
fewer than one person per square
mile but makes up for it in charm.

RESOURCES

**North Park Chamber of
Commerce**
416 4th Street
Walden, CO 80480
970-723-4600
www.northparkchamber.com

North Park Visitors Bureau
427 Main Street
Walden, CO 80480
970-723-4600
www.northparkvisitorsbureau.com

NEW ROUTE

**The route has changed here to go
through Hot Sulphur Springs on
quieter roads, via US 40**

PLACES TO STAY

Canyon Motel
221 Byers Avenue
Hot Sulphur Springs, CO 80451
970-725-3395
$$

Hot Springs Resort & Spa
5609 Spring Rd
Hot Sulphur Springs, CO 80451
800-510-6235, 970-725-3306
$$$

CAMPING

Pioneer State Park
Just off US 40 & Park Street.
Wildlife area.

Thermal pool, West Thumb Geyser Basin, Yellowstone National Park, Wyoming.

WYOMING
8 Days – 462.5 Miles

The border between Colorado and Wyoming isn't geographically very distinct, the same glorious North Park region of the Platte River, an infinite meadow surrounded on four sides by magnificent mountains. The roads, however, are a completely different story. Precisely at the border, Colorado's crumbling cow paths with their nonexistent shoulders turned instantly into silky smooth roads with wide shoulders. We felt like we were sailing a magic carpet into Wyoming. No traffic, just soaring red-tailed hawks and lots of antelope—actually 50 percent of the country's antelope reside in Wyoming, so they say.

WYOMING FACTS & RESOURCES

Fast Facts:
Population: 453,000
Capital: Cheyenne
Nickname: Cowboy State
Flower: Indian Paintbrush
Bird: Meadowlark
Tree: Cottonwood

Dates in History:
1843 "Great migration" along the Oregon Trail begins
1868 Wyoming Territory created
1890 Enters Union
1925 Nellie Tayloe Ross first woman governor in country

Wyoming Division of Tourism
561 High Plains Drive
Cheyenne, WY 82002
307-777-7777

Wyoming State Parks, Historic Sites & Trails
Barrett Building, 4th Flr
2301 Central Ave
Cheyenne, WY 82002
307-777-6323
wyoparks.state.wy.us

Today you'll ride 51 miles without services with a wide open road, big shoulder and little traffic. It's wonderful biking, especially with a tail wind. At about 33 miles you'll make a 2.5- mile climb but then there's a 3.5- mile downhill that makes it all worthwhile. The first "town" you get to is Riverside on the Encampment River. Encampment itself is a little further down the road but the real action is in Riverside with numerous cabins, taverns and small groceries.

PLACES TO STAY

Bear Trap Cafe & Cabins
120 E Riverside Avenue
Riverside, WY 82325
307-327-5277
$

Lazy Acres Campground & Motel
110 Fields Avenue
Riverside, WY 82325
307-327-5968
$ 🔲

Vacher's Bighorn Lodge
508 McCaffrey Avenue
Encampment, WY 82325
307-327-5110
$$

CAMPING

Lazy Acres Campground & Motel
110 Fields Avenue
Riverside, WY 82325
307-327-5968

Grand View Park
6th Street
Encampment, WY 82325
307-327-5501
Restrooms, water, no showers.
Next to museum.

Saratoga Lake Campground
307-326-8335

Bear Trap Cafe & Bar
120 E Riverside Avenue
Riverside, WY 82325
307-327-5277
Hotcakes for the hungry biker.

Mangy Moose Saloon
108 Riverside Ave
Encampment, WY 82325
307-327-5117

SPECIAL INTEREST

Stoney Creek Outfitters
216 E Walnut
Saratoga, WY 82331
307-326-8750
www.GRMO.com
Everything for the hungry fly fisherperson.

Grand Encampment Museum
807 Barnett Ave
Encampment, WY 82325
307-327-5308
Known best for its two-story outhouse.

You'll spend today cruising through the high plains of Wyoming, like riding on top of a gigantic flying saucer. Coyotes, jack rabbits, badgers, prairie dogs and pronghorn deer all share the road. First coffee stop is at 18 miles in Saratoga. The Wolcot Convenience Store is 39 miles from Encampment.

Rawlins, once a booming cowboy and mining town, now hosts the Cowboy Poetry Gathering in July. You'll pass the Sinclair Oil Refinery with its green dinosaur logo at 53 miles. Rawlins is sandwiched between a freeway intersection at the east end of town and another one at the west end. Both ends are thriving with new convenience stores, restaurants, retail and hotels. The old center of town is still nice, hanging on, thanks to another Main Street America grant. Its library, post office, gift and sporting goods stores all quietly snooze along.

PLACES TO STAY

Best Western Cottontree Inn
2221 W Spruce Street
Rawlins, WY 82301
800-780-7234, 307-324-2737
$$ 🚐 🍽 🏊 🖳

Super 8 Motel
2338 Wagon Circle Street
Rawlins, WY 82301
307-328-0630, 800-536-0719
$ 🚐
Near the Best Western.

Bit O' Country B&B
Closed.

CAMPING

American President's Campground
2346 W Spruce Street
Rawlins, WY 82301
307-324-3218, 800-294-3218
Western Hills Campground
2500 Wagon Circle Road
Rawlins, WY 82301
307-324-2592

FOOD & DINING

Food In Route:
Su Casa Restaurant
705 Lincoln Ave
Sinclair, WY 82301
307-328-1745
Half a mile beyond the Sinclair
Oil Refinery, 6 miles from
Rawlins. Reputedly the best
Mexican restaurant for miles.

SPECIAL INTEREST

Overland Trail Marker
At 29 miles.Used by the westward
immigrants and the famous
Overland Stage, 1861-1868.

Carbon County Cowboy Poetry
Gathering – July
307-326-8855
www.wyomingcowboypoetry.com
Held in Encampment.

RESOURCES

Rawlins Carbon County
Chamber of Commerce
519 W Cedar Street
Rawlins, WY 82301
307-324-4111

Wyoming Tourist Information
800-225-5996

Bed & Breakfast Inns & Guest
Ranches of Wyoming
www.WyomingBnB-RanchRec.
com

On today's ride you'll be biking through a geological textbook. After crossing the Continental Divide, you'll coast down onto the smooth, prehistoric sea bottom of the Great Divide Basin, deposited 350 million years ago. At 4 miles there's the Paint Mine Historic Site, source of the "hematite" used in "Rawlin's Red" to paint the Brooklyn Bridge. Plan to stop at Grandma's Cafe (33 miles) for oversized pancakes. At about 43 miles there's a very welcome shady rest area courtesy of the Department of Transportation. Along the way you'll see Split Rock, a major historic site marking the convergence of the Oregon Trail (1812-1869), the Mormon Trail (1846-1847), and the Pony Express (1860-1862).

Jeffrey City isn't a city at all; it's a ghost town. Started in 1971 with a big uranium strike, the town expanded to 5-6,000 population, but when 3 Mile Island happened, the town went bust.

PLACES TO STAY

Call the Split Rock Bar & Cafe Camping may be the only option.

CAMPING

Lions Club Pavilion
Jeffrey City, WY 82310

FOOD & DINING

Split Rock Bar & Cafe
2297 Hwy 789
Jeffrey City, WY 82310
307-544-2223
Call ahead. Near the Coates Motel. The only restaurant for miles.

Food In Route:

Pack supplies - you're out of luck.

Split Rock Historic Site
National Register of Historic Places. Three trails used this landmark for navigation.
First wagon train rolled through Split Rock in 1841.
Brigham Young led the first Mormon Wagon Train west through this area in 1846.

The Pony Express Route (1860-62)
Only in operation for 18 months, the Pony Express employed 500 ponies and 80 riders, including such notables as Buffalo Bill Cody. Each rider rode 70 miles round trip, taking 10 days to cross the West. They carried the mail in a "Mochila" leather pouch. Postage for a single letter was $1 to $5. October 24, 1861, brought an end to the Pony Express with the invention of the telegraph, but the trail is still in evidence today at Split Rock.

The former one and only Top Hat Motel in Jeffrey City, WY

This is flat, empty country populated mostly by sage grouse, pronghorn and moose. From Jeffrey City the first coffee stop is at 19 miles in Sweetwater Station and opens at 8 a.m. This site, also called the "Sixth Crossing," while in Sweetwater you may see the handcarts pulled by Mormons on pilgrimages along the Mormon Trail. At 19 miles you begin a long climb up Beaver Divide and then enjoy a well-deserved 5 mile downhill. At 45 miles you'll get your first glimpse of the "Red Rocks" of Wyoming.

Known as the "City of Bronze" for its bronze foundry and numerous oversized wildlife statues, Lander was selected the fifth best small town in America by *Good Morning America*.

PLACES TO STAY

Pronghorn Lodge – Budget Host
150 E Main
Lander, WY 82520
800-BUDHOST, 307-332-3940
www.pronghornlodge.com
$$ 🖵

Downtown Motel
569 Main Street
Lander, WY 82520
307-332-3171
$$ 🏊

CAMPING

Lander City Park
405 Freemont Street
Lander, WY 82520
307-332-4647

Holiday Lodge "Riverside" Camping
210 McFarlane Drive
Lander, WY 82520
307-332-2511
$5. Full use of pool and spa.

Sleeping Bear RV
715 E Main Street
Lander, WY 82520
307-332-5159
Great place!

Food In Route:
Rick & Mattie Wilmes
Sweetwater Station
418 Hwy 287
Sweetwater, WY 82520
307-544-2322
Mormon Trail handcarts often
pass by here.

The Oxbow Restaurant
170 E Main
Lander, WY 82520
307-332-0233
Next door to the Pronghorn
Lodge. Big salads.

Lander Bar & Grill
126 Main Street
Lander, WY 82520
307-332-7009
www.landerbar.com
Outdoor dining, great beer and
pizza.

Cowfish Restaurant
148 Main Street
Lander, WY 82520
307-332-8227
Best beer on the Trans Am!

SPECIAL INTEREST

Ice Slough
10 miles beyond Jeffrey City.
In the 1880s when traveling
immigrants needed ice, they cut
blocks that were frozen under the
peat bog at Ice Slough.

"Wind River Country"
www.windriver.org

RESOURCES

Lander Chamber of Commerce
800-433-0662, 307-332-3892
www.landerchamber.org

**Fremont County Carnegie
Library**
200 Armorreti Street
Lander, WY 82520
307-332-5194
Computers with internet access.

Today's route travels through the 2.4-million-acre Wind River Indian Reservation, historical home of the Shoshone and more recently the Arapaho. At 27 miles is the top of Bighorn Ridge, where Bighorn Flats houses the world's largest population of Bighorn Sheep. 14 miles before Dubois, you'll leave the reservation and enter the spectacular Red Rocks area.

Dubois is a great little cowboy town known for its dude ranches and super Chamber of Commerce.

Note: Days 54 and 55 are both fairly long and have significant elevation gains. If you prefer to break this portion of the trip into three days, you can stop at Early Ranch or Red Rock today, Pinnacle Buttes tomorrow and then glide into Colter Bay on the thrid day. See "In Route" options for accommodations. They are constantly changing.

PLACES TO STAY

Black Bear Country Inn
505 N Ramshorn Street
Dubois, WY 82513
307-455-3455, 303-842-2315
$

Branding Iron Inn
401 W Ramshorn Street
Dubois, WY 82513
307-455-2893
$

In Route:

Red Rock RV Park & Campground
14 miles before Dubois.
Currently closed but check with Dubois Chamber: 307-455-2556.

CAMPING

Dubois/Wind River KOA
225 Welty Street, US 26/287
Dubois, WY 82513
307-455-2238

Riverside Inn & Campground
5810 US Hwy 26
Dubois, WY 82513
307-455-2337
1 mile East of Dubois

FOOD & DINING

Food In Route:
Hines General Store
14597 US 287
Fort Washakie, WY 82514
307-332-3278
Open 7 days a week; picnic tables.

Crowheart Store
8526 US26
Crowheart, WY
307-486-2285
45 miles. Grocery store.

Cowboy Cafe
115 E Ramshorn Street
Dubois, WY 82513
307-455-2595
Great breakfast for cowboy bikers.

SPECIAL INTEREST

Wind River Indian Reservation
Wyoming's only Indian
reservation with 2.4 million acres.

Wind River Trading Post &
Gallery of the Wind Museum
US Hwy 287 & Trout Rd
Fort Washakie, WY 82514
307-332-3267

Crowheart Butte Marker 1866
At 41 miles, this marker
commemorates the Crow and
Shoshone fight for supremacy of
the Wind River hunting grounds.
Chief Washakie allegedly cut
out the heart of a Crow warrior
and carried it on his lance at the
victorious war dance.

Wyoming Wool Works
1508 Highview Drive
Dubois, WY 82513
307-455-2858
Email: *wyowool@wyoming.com*
100 percent Wyoming wool
blankets from co-op members.
Across from Cowboy Cafe.

National Bighorn Sheep
Interpretive Center
907 W Ramshorn
Dubois, WY 82513
888-209-2795, 307-455-3429
www.bighorn.org

RESOURCES

Dubois Chamber of Commerce
PO Box 632
616 W Ramshorn Street
Dubois, WY 82513
307-455-2556
www.duboiswyomingchamber.org

Get ready for another little hill: up and over Togwotee Pass at 9,638 feet for your fourth crossing of the Continental Divide. On this day my husband sighed, "I thought we were going to cross the Rockies, not take up permanent residence in them." Tie Hack Memorial (17 miles) and Pinnacle Buttes (20 miles) make nice rest stops along the climb. At 30 miles you finally cross Togwotee Pass and scoot happily downhill for 17 fast miles. Stop for pancakes at Cowboy Village & Resort on your way to Colter Bay. Once you arrive at Grand Teton National Park (54 miles), you'll pay an entry fee at the park gate. The views of the Teton Range are inspiring at any hour.

PLACES TO STAY

In Route (If you're dividing days 54 and 55 into three days).

Pinnacle Buttes Lodge & Campground
3577 US Hwy 26 W
Dubois, WY 82513
307-455-2506
$$ ✗
20 miles west of Dubois.
Temporarily out-of-business.

Colter Bay Village Cabins
Colter Bay Village,
Grand Teton National Park, WY
800-628-9988
$✗▣

Jackson Lake Lodge
101 Jackson Lake Lodge Rd
Moran, WY 83013
307-543-2811
$$$$ ▯≈✗▣
6 miles south of Colter Bay.

CAMPING

Colter Bay Tent Village
Colter Bay Village
Grand Teton National Park, WY
307-543-2811 x1080,
307-543-2828

Colter Bay Campground
Reservations: 800-628-9988
or 307-543-2811

FOOD & DINING

Colter Bay Indian Arts Museum
307-739-3594

RESOURCES

Food In Route:
Wilderness Boundary Restaurant
Lava Mountain Lodge
3577 US Hwy 26 W
Dubois, WY 82513
307-455-2506
Saturday nights, Dutch-oven
cooking over an open fire. Even
the cobbler is done in the Dutch-
oven. Worth the stop. 20 miles
west of Dubois. Check first.

Grand Teton Lodge Company.
800-628-9988, 307-543-2811
Information and lodging
reservations.

Colter Bay Visitor Center
Colter Bay Marine Rd
Grand Teton National Park
Colter Bay Village, WY 83013
307-739-3594

Togwotee Mountain Lodge
Grizzly Grill
On top of Togwotee Pass
16.5 miles east of Moran at
Junction US 26/287
Moran, WY 83013
307-543-2847, 866-278-4245

NPS National Parks Service
307-739-3300, 307-739-3501

Take your time today; it's
gorgeous country despite the
Winnebagos. Enjoy the scenery
but be sure to bike carefully.

John Colter Cafe Court
Colter Bay Village
Grand Teton National Park, WY
307-543-2811
Burgers, hot dogs, deli
sandwiches.

*Dutch-oven cooking at the Wild Bunch
at Pinnacle Buttes Lodge & Campground
outside of Dubois, Wyoming*

Colter Bay General Store
Colter Bay Village
Grand Teton National Park, WY
Open daily.

You'll start the day cycling around Jackson Lake. At 9 miles you'll pass Lizzard Creek Campground and then at 12 miles begin the John D. Rockefeller Parkway. At 17 miles there's a relatively new coffee stop at the Flagg Ranch Resort, with a grocery and dining room. The Yellowstone Park entrance is at 19 miles; so the last half of the day is filled with views of Yellowstone, the world's first National Park and still one of our most impressive. At 37 miles you'll cross the Continental Divide for the fifth time.

PLACES TO STAY

Grant Village Hotel
Yellowstone National Park, WY
307-344-7311
www.yellowstonenationalparklodges.com

CAMPING

Grant Village Campground
307-344-7311
www.travelyellowstone.com

FOOD & DINING

Food In Route:
Sheffields Restaurant & Bar
In between Grand Teton and Yellowstone National Parks
800-443-2311, 307-543-2356

Grant Village Restaurant
Grant Village, WY
Reservations for fine dining required.
866-439-7375, 307-344-7311

SPECIAL INTEREST

Grant Bay Visitor Center
307-344-2650
Open daily 8 a.m. to 7 p.m. Information, exhibits, video of role of fire in Yellowstone. Naturalist lectures.

Yellowstone National Park
307-344-7381
www.nps.gov/yell
- Second largest national park in
the contiguous US
- World's greatest concentration of
thermal features
- Home to largest concentration
of elk in the world
- World's largest petrified forest

Bike through the park early in the morning to preserve the peace and increase your chances at seeing bison, elk, and coyote along the roadside. Take your time again today since the views are spectacular. At 6.7 miles you'll cross the Continental Divide for the sixth time, then again at 12 miles. At 20 miles turn right onto Old Faithful Parkway and cruise into the Old Faithful Lodge, built in 1904. Settle in on the rooftop deck while sipping an espresso as Old Faithful makes its scheduled debut. Later in the day you'll pass many burbling geysers, including Midway and Fountain Paint Pot. At 32 miles is the Nez Perce Campaign Marker where Chief Joseph had the grace to let a group of Yellowstone tourists pass as he was fleeing the US Cavalry in 1877. After that you'll head west along the famous Madison River, fly-fishing paradise, on your way to West Yellowstone, a lively tourist town with plenty of services.

PLACES TO STAY

Best Western Desert Inn
133 N Canyon Street
West Yellowstone, MT 59758
406-646-7376
$$

Yellowstone Westgate Hotel
638 Madison Avenue
West Yellowstone, MT 59758
406-646-4212
$$

The Historic Madison Hotel
139 Yellowstone Avenue
West Yellowstone, MT 59758
406-646-7745
E-mail:
madisonhotel@wyellowstone.com

CAMPING

The first two campgrounds are located in town:

Pony Express RV Park
4 Firehole Avenue
West Yellowstone, MT 59758
800-217-4613, 406-823-6961
www.yellowstonevacations.com

Yellowstone Grizzly RV Park
210 S Electric Street
West Yellowstone, MT 59758
406-646-4466

Rustic Wagon Campground
637 Hwy 20
West Yellowstone. MY 59758
406-646-7387

Madison Junction Campground
307-344-7381
Inside the Park. 14 miles before
West Yellowstone.

FOOD & DINING

Bulwinkle's Saloon & Restaurant
115 N Canyon Street
West Yellowstone, MT 59758
406-646-7974
West Yellowstone's best bar.

Mountain Mike's Cafe
38 Canyon
West Yellowstone, MT 59758
406-646-9462
Great selection of Montana beer
and wine.

SPECIAL INTEREST

Old Faithful Visitor Center
Yellowstone National Park, WY
307-545-2751
Open daily 9 a.m. – 5 p.m. Old
Faithful Geyser eruption schedule
and film.

RESOURCES

West Yellowstone Chamber of Commerce
30 Yellowstone Avenue
West Yellowstone, MT 59758
406-646-7701
www.destinationyellowstone.com

Free Heel & Wheel Bike Shop
40 Yellowstone Avenue
West Yellowstone, MT 59758
406-646-7744

Madison River Outfitters
117 Canyon Street
West Yellowstone, MT 59758
800-646-9644, 406-646-9644
www.madisonriveroutfitters.com

Yellowstone County Van Tours
406-646-9310
Excellent way to see the park that
is not on route, on a rest day.

MONTANA
6 Days - 334.5 Miles

The name *Montana* comes from the Spanish word *montana*, meaning mountain. It is aptly named. With the soaring Rockies, the Bitterroots, spectacular mountain valleys and lovely high prairies, this is a great state for bicycling. It's also a pretty good state for fishing, too, if you're so inclined. You'll ride through historic Virginia City and the Big Hole National Monument to the college town of Missoula and onward to lovely Lolo Pass and eventually Idaho.

MONTANA FACTS & RESOURCES

Fast Facts
Population: 799,000
Capital: Helena
Nickname: Big Sky Country
Flower: Bitterroot
Bird: Western Meadowlark
Tree: Ponderosa Pine

Dates in History
1805 Lewis and Clark arrive in Montana
1862 Miners strike gold
1876 Battle of Little Big Horn

Travel Montana
301 S Park Avenue
PO Box 200533
Helena, MT 59620
800-847-4868
www.visitmt.com

DAY 58 WEST YELLOWSTONE TO ENNIS, MT Pop: 773 people; 773,000 trout
Mileage: 73
Est. Elevation: -1,600
AC Map: 4:46, 45, 44

This is some of the best biking on the whole trip. (We keep saying that, don't we?) Today it's 73 miles along the Madison River and mostly downhill. The first 20 miles are along Hebgen Lake, site of the August 1959 earthquake, which hit 7.5 on the Richter scale. The story unfolds at 22 miles at the Hebgen Dam, "the dam that held." A mile later you'll come to Refuge Point, where 250 people were trapped by the quake and had to be helicoptered out to safety. At 28.5 miles you'll learn more at the Earthquake Visitor's Center. Throughout the rest of the day you'll see numerous "put-ins" and "take-outs" for drift boats plying the world-famous Madison River.

Ennis is located in the Madison Valley, a spot mostly known for its fly fishing. It also has four espresso stands, good restaurants and many antique shops.

PLACES TO STAY

Riverside Motel
346 Main Street
Ennis, MT 59729
406-682-4240, 800-535-4139
$$

El Western Resort & Motel
Ennis, MT 59729
800-831-2773, 406-682-4217
www.elwestern.com
$$$ ✗
.5 miles out of town on Hwy 287.

CAMPING

Ennis Village RV
15 Geyser Street
Ennis, MT 59729
406-682-5272
Hwy 287, East of Ennis
Toilets, water, boat launch,
US Forest Service.

Cameron Store & Campground
Hwy 287
Cameron, MT
406-682-7744
Coffee stop, cabins, camping,
and RV park.

FOOD & DINING

Food In Route:
Cameron Store & Campground
Hwy 287
Cameron, MT
406-682-7744
Coffee stop, cabins, RV park.

Yesterday's Restaurant & Soda Fountain
124 Main Street
Ennis, MT 59729
406-682-4246
Old-fashioned antique marble-topped soda fountain.

Madison Foods
4979 US Hwy 287 N
Ennis, MT 59729
406-682-4306

Claim Jumper Saloon
305 Main Street
Ennis, MT 59729
406-682-5558
Best bar in town.

SPECIAL INTEREST

Randy Brown's Madison Flyfisher
406-682-7481
"Fly fishing the Madison since 1972."

Hebgen Lake Earthquake Center
406-823-6961
Hwy 287 in route to Ennis.

RESOURCES

Ennis Area Chamber of Commerce
201 E Main Street
Ennis, MT 59729
406-682-4388
www.ennischamber.com

Madison Valley Library
210 W Main Street
Ennis, MT 59729
406-682-7244
Internet access, closed Sunday.

Madison Ranger District
5 Forest Service Rd
Ennis, MT 59729
406-682-4253

Dinner on the Madison River

Although today's recommended ride is only 15 miles, the historic Virginia City area is well worth a layover day. The fact that the 15 miles includes a tough 8 mile climb of 2,000-plus feet makes this a reasonable strategy for even non-history buffs. If you don't feel like studying Montana history or are wanting to rack up some miles, this day can be combined with the next one for a total of 72 miles and 3,000-plus feet. Shortly after leaving Ennis you'll start climbing, reaching a summit overlooking the Madison River Valley at about 10 miles. From there it's a pleasant glide into gold rush country.

Charming Virginia City was the site of a fevered Montana gold rush from 1863 to 1865. Designated a National Historic Landmark in 1961, the city once included over 1,000 buildings. Although only 237 buildings remain today, there are excellent places to stay and eat, historic tours, two museums and even the chance to ride the local fire engine or historic Alder Gulch railroad.

PLACES TO STAY

Bennett House Country Inn
115 E Idaho
Virginia City, MT 59755
877-843-5220, 406-843-5220
www.bennetthouseinn.com
$$ ☕

Stonehouse Inn B&B
306 E Idaho
Virginia City, MT 59755
406-843-5504
$$ ☕

Fairweather Inn & Nevada City Hotel
Virginia City, MT
800-829-2969, 406-843-5377
$$
1.3 miles down US 287.

CAMPING

Virginia City RV Park
1302 E Wallace, Hwy 287
Virginia City, MT 59755
406-843-5493
E-mail: *vcamp@3rivers.net*

FOOD & DINING

Star Bakery Restaurant
1576 US Hwy
Virginia City, MT 59755
406-843-5777
Open 7 a.m. for breakfast.

Virginia City Cafe
210 Wallace St
Virginia City, MT 59755
406-843-5511
Homemade breads and cookies.

Roadmaster Grille
124 W Wallace St
Virginia City, MT 59755
406-843-5234
"Full service garage" restaurant,
car booths.

SPECIAL INTEREST

Walking Guide to Virginia City
Montana Heritage Commission
Virginia City, MT 59755
406-843-5247, 800-829-2969

Alder Gulch Short Line Railroad
Virginia City, MT 59755
406-843-5247
Steam engines make a short round
trip between Virginia City and
Nevada City along Alder Gulch,
site of Montana's greatest placer
gold rush in the spring of 1863.

**Thompson-Hickman Memorial
Museum**
220 Wallace Street
Virginia City, MT
406-843-5238

Nevada City
1.5 miles West on SR 287
800-829-2969

RESOURCES

**Virginia City Chamber of
Commerce**
800-829-2969

You'll begin the day spinning down the Ruby and Beaverhead Valleys, meeting an occasional car and accompanied by pronghorn antelope running beside the road. Montana mornings shine through split-rail fences with stunning mountainous backdrops. At 19 miles is the town of Sheridan with a great bakery and cafe. Later there's a coffee stop in the small town of Twin Bridges at about 28 miles. This is Lewis and Clark territory. You'll see the famous Beaverhead Rock 15 miles before Dillon, the point where young Sacajawea recognized her surroundings and thus paved the way for the expedition's correct route west toward Lemhi Pass, the Rockies and the Bitterroots. You'll probably remember this landmark for a long time yourself.

PLACES TO STAY

Best Western Paradise Inn
650 N Montana Street
Dillon, MT 59725
406-683-4214
$$ 🚪✕🏊

Comfort Inn of Dillon
450 N Interchange
Dillon, MT 59725
800-442-6423, 406-683-6831
$$ 🚪🏊

America's Best Value Inn
550 N Montana Street
Dillon, MT 59725
406-683-4288
$$

CAMPING

Dillon KOA Campground
735 W Park
Dillon, MT 59725
406-683-2749

**Sky Line Trailer Court
& Campground**
3525 Hwy 91 N
Dillon, MT 59725
406-683-4692
2.5 miles North on old US 91.
Private campground.

FOOD & DINING

Food In Route:
Blue Anchor Bar & Cafe
102 N Main St
Twin Bridges, MT 59754
406-684-5655
Great place for breakfast 28 miles
from Virginia City.

Best Western Paradise Inn &
Joker Lounge
660 N Montana Street
Dillon, MT 59725
406-683-9949
Slot machines in the bar.

SPECIAL INTEREST

Beaverhead Rock
406-834-3413
15 miles East of Dillon.
Sacajawea's landmark.

Beaverhead County Museum
15 S Montana Street
Dillon, MT 59725
406-683-5027
Open Monday - Saturday.

RESOURCES

Bad Beaver Bike Shop
Unfortunately out of business.
Check with the Chamber for
nearest bike shop.

Beaverhead Chamber of
Commerce
10 W Reeder Street
Dillon, MT 59725
406-683-5511
www.beaverheadchamber.com

Alternative Bike & Board Shop
250 S Montana Street
Dillon, MT 59725
Erratic hours, call ahead.
406-683-5160

DAY 61 DILLON TO JACKSON or WISDOM
Pop: 50
Mileage: 47.5 to Jackson; 65.5 to Wisdom
Est. Elevation: 3,000
AC Map: 4:41, 40, 39

The glorious Big Hole Valley – also known as "Bighole Basin," "Big Hole Prairie," "Land of the Big Snows" and "Land of 10,000 Haystacks"– was considered a wilderness for several decades before the Bitterroot and Beaverhead Valleys were settled. You'll climb two passes today: Badger (6,760 feet) and Big Hole Pass (7,360 feet) on your way to Jackson Hot Springs where Lewis and Clark once camped in 1806. And yes, there are still great hot springs available for soaking. If you're feeling energetic (or get water-logged easily), Wisdom is a reasonable 18 miles away.

PLACES TO STAY
JACKSON, Pop:50

Jackson Hot Springs Lodge Restaurant & Bar
108 Jardine Ave
Jackson, MT 59736
406-834-3151
$$$ 🚪 ✕ 〰
www.jacksonhotsprings.com

PLACES TO STAY
WISDOM, Pop: 200

Nez Perce Motel
509 Montana 43
Wisdom, MT 59761
406-689-3254
$$
18 miles from Jackson.

CAMPING

Jackson Hot Springs Lodge Restaurant & Bar
108 Jardine Ave
Jackson, MT 59736
406-834-3151
www.jacksonhotsprings.com
Has tent space in back of property for bikers. Hot springs available.

American Legion Park
Wisdom, MT 59761
Across Big Hole River Bridge on the SR 43.

FOOD & DINING

JACKSON

**Jackson Hot Springs Lodge
Restaurant & Bar**
108 Jardine Ave
Jackson, MT 59736
406-834-3151
Romantic restaurant. Super bar.

Jackson Mercantile
Jackson, MT 59736
406-834-3264
www.bigholevalley.com
Limited groceries.

FOOD & DINING

WISDOM

Big Hole Crossing Restaurant
105 Park Street
Wisdom, MT 59761
406-689-3800
Open 7 days a week, breakfast,
lunch and dinner. Run by Diane
and daughters.

Wisdom Market
Main Street
Wisdom, MT 59761
406-689-3271
Real groceries.

Historic photo of Wisdom, Montana, by John Vachon - found on an internet search

The route continues in the ever-widening Big Hole Valley through Wisdom to the Big Hole Battlefield National Monument. This site tells the compelling story of Chief Joseph's decision to flee America for the safety and sanctuary of Canada while being chased by the US military through the Bitterroot Valley in 1877. After the battlefield you'll climb both Chief Joseph and Lost Trail Passes, the latter sporting a bathroom and visitor center. After gliding through the Bitterroot Canyon, at 64 miles you'll pass the Trapper Peak Site, where it is thought the Salish Indians resided for 8,000 years. Then you continue down river towards Darby, in the Bitterroot Valley, a charming western town similar to Ennis with fly fishing on the Bitterroot River.

PLACES TO STAY

SULA
Lost Trail Hot Springs Resort
283 Lost Trail Hot Springs Rd
Sula, MT 59871
406-821-3574
$$ ✕ ⚓
Approximately 52 miles from Jackson. The next day is 90 miles to Missoula if you start here.

Sula Country Store & Resort
7060 US Hwy 93 S
Sula, MT 59871
406-821-3364
$
Sleeping cabins, cafe, camping, grocery. 18 miles before Darby.

FOOD & DINING

Food In Route:
Lost Trail Hot Spring Resorts Restaurant & Bar
283 Lost Trail Hot Springs Rd
Sula, MT 59871
406-821-3574

Sula Country Store & Resort
7060 US Hwy 93 S
Sula, MT 59871
406-821-3364
Convenience store and small cafe.

PLACES TO STAY

DARBY

Mountain Spirit Inn
308 S Main Street
Darby, MT 59829
406-821-2405
$
Cabins and campground.

Bud & Shirley's Motel
Main Street
Darby, MT 59829
406-821-3401
$ ✖

CAMPING

Mountain Spirit Inn
308 S Main Street
Darby, MT 59829
406-821-3405
$
Cabins and campground.

Bitterroot Family Campground
406-363-2430
Hamilton, MT 59840
8 miles beyond Darby.

FOOD & DINING

Bud & Shirley's Restaurant
Main Street
Darby, MT 59829
406-821-3401
Lunch and dinner buffet. Open 7
days a week. Breakfast buffet on
weekends.

SPECIAL INTEREST

The Indians in the area dug and
ate the roots of the Bitterroot
flower, thus prompting the
names of the Bitterroot River
and Mountains. Bitterroot is the
Montana state flower.

Big Hole National Battlefield
16425 Hwy 43
Wisdom, MT 59761
406-689-3157, 3155
www.nps.gov\biho

Darby Historic Visitor Center
712 N Main Street
Darby, MT 59829
406-821-1774, 406-821-3913
Ranger station next door. Open 7
days a week 8:30 a.m. – 4:30 p.m.

Darby Library
101 S Marshall Rd
Darby, MT 59829
406-821-4771
Internet access. Open 1-5 p.m.
Monday - Friday.

RESOURCES

**Bitterroot Valley Chamber of
Commerce**
105 E Main St
Hamilton, MT 59840
406-363-2400
www.bitterrootchamber.com
E-mail: *localinfo@bvchamber.com*

Editor's note: New routing to Missoula.

Today you'll continue down the Bitterroot Valley. Closer to Missoula you'll see evidence of the principal local industry, building log cabins. The AC route continues through the now expansive Bitterroot Valley. You'll pass Lolo, where you'll be returning on your way to Idaho. Once closer to the city, follow the AC map through town to the world headquarters of Adventure Bicycling Association on Pine Street. The people are terrific and the ice cream tasty.

PLACES TO STAY

Holiday Inn Parkside
200 S Pattee
Missoula, MT 59802
406-721-8550, 800-399-0408
$$ 🜕 ✕ 🌊

Comfort Inn
1021 E Broadway
Missoula, MT 59802
406-549-7600
$$$$ 🜕

America's Best Value Inn
420 W Broadway
Missoula, MT 59802
888-315-2378

Bel Air Motel
300 E Broadway
Missoula, MT 59802
406-543-3183
$

City Center Motel
338 E Broadway
Missoula, MT 59802
406-543-3183
$

CAMPING

KOA Campground
3450 Tina Avenue
Missoula, MT 59808
800-562-5366, 406-549-0881
Off Reserve Street

FOOD & DINING

Waterfront Pasta House & Ice Cream
809 E Front Street
Missoula, MT 59802
406-549-8826
Gourmet pasta dishes and patio dining with riverfront views.

The Depot
201 W Railroad
Missoula, MT 59802
406-728-7007
Historical location. Salad bar and patio seating.

Bernice's Bakery
190 S Third W
Missoula, MT 59801
406-728-1358
Espresso and goodies. A local hang-out.

SPECIAL INTEREST

Adventure Cycling Association Headquarters
150 E Pine Street
Missoula, MT 59802
800-755-2453, 406-721-1776
www.adventurecycling.org
E-mail:*info@adventurecycling.org*
The hub of cycling, the offices feature many photographs from the original summer of 1976 Bikecentennial and selections from the National Bicycling Touring Portrait Collection. Also on display is Jim and Linda Richardson's (co-founders) Gitane tandem, the first bicycle to cross

the TransAmTrail. Complimentary refreshments available.

University of Montana
Missoula, MT 59802
406-243-0211
www.umt.edu
Internet access.

Historical Museum At Fort Missoula
3400 Captain Rawn Way
Missoula, MT 59804
406-728-3476
Call for directions.
The fort was established in 1877 at the height of the conflict with the Nez Perce and Chief Joseph. Guided tours.

RESOURCES

Open Road Bicycles
517 S Orange Street
Missoula, MT 59802
406-549-2453

Bike Doctor
1101 Toole Avenue
Missoula, MT 59802
406-721-5357

Big Sky Cyclery
1110 South Avenue W
Missoula, MT 59802
406-543-3331

Missoula Bicycle Works
708 S Higgins Avenue
Missoula, MT 59802
406-721-6525

Missoula Chamber of Commerce
825 E Front Street
Missoula, MT 59802
800-526-3465, 406-543-6623
www.exploremissoula.com
www.missoulachamber.com
Open Monday – Friday 8 a.m. to
7 p.m., Saturday 10 a.m. to 6 p.m.

**Missoula Convention & Visitor
Bureau**
101 E Main St
Missoula, MT 59802
800-526-3465, 406-532-3250
www.destinationmissoula.org

Photo: Greg Siple, Adventure Cycling

IDAHO
6 Days - 347 Miles to Oregon

Remote and rugged, Idaho is a wilderness treat for the cyclist. Wild rivers carve their way through the mountain landscapes. Somehow you can almost see Meriwether Lewis and William Clark making their trek over Lolo Pass or launching their canoes on the Snake river. Your trek heads toward Oregon through canyons and creeks, raging rivers and untouched forests. Aptly called the Gem State, Idaho is still a hidden gem waiting to be discovered.

IDAHO FACTS & RESOURCES

Fast Facts
Population: 1.3 million
Capital: Boise
Nickname: The Gem State
Flower: Syringa
Bird: Mountain Bluebird
Tree: White Pine

Idaho Department of Commerce
Idaho Travel Council
PO Box 83720
Boise, ID 83720
1-800-VISIT-ID
208-334-2470
www.visitid.org

Idaho's Hwy 12 – North Central Idaho
www.idahohighway12.com
Traveler's bulletin boards, campground guide, events, weekly updates.
Lewis & Clark in Idaho
www.lewisandclarkidaho.org

Dates in History
1805 Lewis & Clark explore Idaho
1874 Railroad arrives
1890 Idaho 43rd State

Previous Page: Lolo Pass Photo Credit Greg Siple, Adventure Cycling

Once you get out of town, you'll love the very scenic ride along Lolo Creek, following the Nee Mee Poo Trail and up a gradual ascent to Lolo Pass, which separates Montana from Idaho. Along the way you'll pass Fort Fizzle where, in 1887, the US Army attempted to block the flight of the Nez Perce Indians. At Lolo Hot Springs Resort, Cafe & Museum, the grade steepens to 6 to 7 percent. There are many historical trail markers for Lewis and Clark and the Nez Perce Indians, and you'll be making your final crossing of the Continental Divide at the Lolo Summit, 5,235 feet. Lewis and Clark camped here September 13, 1805, in the middle of a snow storm. Reset your watch for the time zone change from Mountain to Pacific time as you cruise downhill to Lochsa Lodge on the delightful Lochsa River.

PLACES TO STAY

Lochsa Lodge & Camping
115 Powell Rd
Lolo, MT 59847
208-942-3405
$✗
Groceries available. 12 miles southwest of Lolo Pass.

Powell USFS Campground
Just down the road from
Lochsa Lodge
208-942-3113

Wendover Campground
15.5 miles southwest of Lolo Pass.
208-842-1234
Showers, $3 per person.

Whitehouse Campground
Near Wendover Campground
Call Powell Ranger Station for
both campgrounds:
208-942-3113.

SPECIAL INTEREST

Fort Fizzle
In July, 1887, the US Army attempted to block the escape of the Nez Perce by using volunteers from Montana. Not wanting to fight with their friendly neighbors, the volunteers all left and Chief Joseph just continued on his way, hence the well-named "Fort Fizzle."

This idyllic route continues through some of Idaho's most beautiful scenery. Once you leave the Powell, you're in Bitterroot country and the route clings to the edge of the cascading Lochsa River, known best for its world-class white water and class 4 rapids. There are no services and no worries for 66 miles, just lots of gorgeous scenery along the river and through the woods. At 14 miles is the Colgate Licks Trailhead and restroom. At 41 miles is the Lochsa Historic Ranger Station and Visitor Center. At 66 miles you'll come to the town of Lowell. Looking Glass Inn is 11 miles beyond, Kooskia 23 miles.

PLACES TO STAY

Three Rivers Resort & Rafting
Hwy 12
Lowell, ID 83539
208-926-4430, 888-926-4430
www.threeriversrafting.com
$$ ✕ ≋
Groceries.

Ryan's Wilderness Inn
8883 Hsy 12
Lowell, ID 83539
208-926-4706
$$ ✕

Reflections Inn
Hwy 12
Kooskia, ID 83539
888-926-0855, 208-926-0855
www.reflectionsinn.com
Email: *ruthmay@reflectionsinn.com*
$$$ ⬧, hot tub
11 miles east of Kooskia, 12 miles west of Lowell. 78.5 miles from Lochsa Lodge.

CAMPING

LOWELL
Three Rivers Resort & Rafting
115 Selway Rd, Lowell, ID 83539
208-926-4430, 888-926-4430
www.threeriversresort.com
$$ ✕ ≋
Groceries.

Wild Goose Campground
208-926-4275
National Forest campground on the banks of the river. 2 miles west of Lowell.

DAY 66 LOWELL or LOOKING GLASS TO GRANGEVILLE, ID Pop. 3,328
Mileage: Lowell 49.5; LG 37.5
Est. Elevation: 2,100
AC Map: 3:31, 30, 29

From Lowell or Looking Glass you'll continue on Hwy 12 towards Kooskia, population 694 and the "Gateway to Idaho's Wilderness." At Kooskia, you'll make a left turn on SR 13, "Idaho's Northwest Passage Scenic Highway," crossing over the middle fork of the Clearwater. Many cyclists stop here for pancakes or homemade pie at the River's Cafe. Once through Kooskia you'll enter the Nez Perce Indian Reservation and travel through a narrow farming valley. At Harpster you'll start a long climb towards Grangeview, a 6 to 7 percent grade for five miles with a 2,000-foot gain. At the crest of the hill you'll enter a plateau typical of central Idaho's rolling wheat country. Grangeville, seat of Idaho County, is a coffee-happy place with at least five espresso stores and many amenities.

PLACES TO STAY

Gateway Inn
700 W Main Street
Grangeville, ID 83530
208-983-2500
$ 🛏☕♨

Super 8 Motel
801 W South 1st Street
Grangeville, ID 83530
208-983-1002, 800-536-0719
$$

Elkhorn Lodge
822 W South 1st Street
Grangeville, ID 83530
208-983-1500
$
Behind the Super 8.

CAMPING

Lion's Club Park
N Myrtle Road
Grangeville, ID 83530
208-983-1351

Riverdance Lodge
7743 US 12
Kooskia, ID 83539
800-451-6034
Cabins, camping, showers, and restaurant.

**Mt. View Mobile Home
& RV Park**
127 Cuningham Street
Grangeville, ID 83530
208-983-2328

FOOD & DINING

**Food In Route:
The River's Cafe**
18 N Main Street
Kooskia, ID 83539
208-926-0986
Great homemade pies and pancakes.

Clearwater Valley Harvest Food
113 N Main
Across from River's
Kooskia, ID 83539
208-926-4242

Palenque Mexican Restaurant
711 W Main Street
Grangeville, ID 83530
208-935-7700
Cold beer and hot nachos.
Famous Palenque Burrito.

Coffee Outlet Espresso
700 W Main
Grangeville, ID 83530
206-983-1911
Delivers espressos.

SPECIAL INTEREST

Nez Perce National Historic Park
208-843-2261
Twenty-eight sites are scattered across this 12,000-square-mile park throughout Idaho, Oregon, Washington and Montana. They recall the impressive history of the Nez Perce Indians, who lived for thousands of years in this area. After many battles with the US Army, the Nez Perce finally surrendered only 40 miles from Canada and were sadly exiled to Oklahoma territory.

Nez Perce Historic Park Site
First major battle of the Nez Perce War in 1877 near White Bird on the Nez Perce Trail.

Blue Fox "Art Deco" Theatre
Main Street
Grangeville, ID 83530

RESOURCES

**Grangeville Area
Chamber of Commerce**
703 W South 1st Street
Grangeville, ID 83530
208-983-0960
www.grangevilleidaho.com

Holiday Sports & Bike Shop
Closed. Was on Main Street.

Today you'll climb the historic Whitebird grade to White Bird Pass. Six miles from Grangeville a marker denotes Camas Prairie where the Nez Perce gathered camas bulbs, an important staple in their diet. This also marks the beginning of a 7 percent, two-mile climb to the summit at 4,245 feet. Approximately one mile past the summit, look for an unmarked but paved road on your left which is the OLD White Bird highway. This scenic alternative offers you a peaceful route downhill through the historic White Bird Canyon. At 19.5 miles the town of White Bird sports a General Store and the Silver Dollar Restaurant. At 24 miles you'll find the Skookumchuck Rest Area on the Salmon River, and you'll follow this river all the way to Riggins.

Riggins, "Rafter's Heaven," is located on the Salmon River and is the headquarters for many different white water activities, if you're so inclined. Outfitters abound.

PLACES TO STAY

Riverview Motel
704 N Hwy 95
Riggins, ID 83549
208-628-3041, 800-256-2322
$$
On the river.

Salmon Rapids Lodge
1010 S Main Street
Riggins, ID 83549
208-628-2743
www.salmonrapids.com
$$$ 🛏🏊🖥

CAMPING

River Village RV Park
1434 N Hwy 95
Riggins, ID 83549
208-628-3443
Showers, laundromat.

FOOD & DINING

**Seven Devils Steakhouse &
Saloon**
312 S Main Street
Riggins, ID 83549
208-628-3358
Open 7 days a week.

SPECIAL INTEREST

**Outfitters and Guided Outdoor
Adventures:**
Brundage Whitewater Adventures
208-628-4212
www.raftbrundage.com

Epley's Whitewater Adventures
208-628-3580
www.epleys.com

Salmon River Challenge
208-628-3264
www.salmonriverchallenge.com

RESOURCES

**Salmon River Chamber of
Commerce**
126 N Main Street
Riggins, ID 83549
208-756-2100, 800-727-2540
Phone rings in the Library where
the chamber is located.

Idaho Travel Council
1-800-VISIT ID

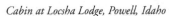

Cabin at Locsha Lodge, Powell, Idaho

DAY 68 RIGGINS TO COUNCIL, ID
Pop: 831
Mileage: 60.5
Est. Elevation: 3,000
AC Map: 3:28, 27, 26, 25

This segment includes a day-long gentle climb at 2 to 3 percent along the Little Salmon River. At 24 miles the route opens up into meadowland, and at 31 miles you'll cross the 45th Parallel, halfway between the Equator and the North Pole, but you're much more than half way to the West Coast. At 49 miles you make a steep end-of-the-day climb at 5 to 7 percent into the town of Council. If you're feeling your oats, you can always continue 22 more miles to Cambridge.

PLACES TO STAY
COUNCIL

Starlite Motel
Hwy 95, 102 N Dartmouth
Council, ID 83612
208-253-4868
$

Old Heartland Inn
Closed

PLACES TO STAY
CAMBRIDGE

Frontier Motel and RV Park
240 S Superior St
Cambridge, ID 83610
208-257-3851
$$
Possible camping.

Hunter's Inn
Hwy 95 & 71 Junction
Cambridge, ID 83610
208-257-3325
$$

CAMPING

Boise Cascade "Old Sawmill Park"
On Galena by City Hall
Council, ID 83612

Chamber of Commerce Park
Michigan & Illinois
Council, ID 83612
208-253-6830
Next to Norm's Corner Pizza.
Restrooms.

Hodges RV Park
415 S Hornet Street
Council, ID 83612
208-253-6042

FOOD & DINING

Ace Saloon
103 Illinois Ave
Council, ID 83612
208-253-4469

RESOURCES

Council Chamber of Commerce
PO Box 527
Council, ID 83612
208-253-6830
www.councilchamberofcommerce.
com

Quiet, rural roads climb and weave through the Weiser River and Pine Creek drainage basins today on your way to renowned Hell's Canyon. At seven miles you'll pass a sign for historic Mesa Orchards, 1910. Fourteen hundred acres of apples lasted in this orchard for more than half a century. The first food stop is at 21 miles near Cambridge. The Gateway Cafe & Store offers a great breakfast and fresh fruit. You'll hit the Summit of the Pine Creek Drainage Area at 4,131 feet and about 39 miles. At 52 miles you'll reach Brownlee Dam and a few miles later, you'll cross the Snake River into Oregon, your last state. Note a change in time zones from Mountain to Pacific. There's a steep end-of-day descent to the Oxbow area.

PLACES TO STAY

Hell's Canyon B&B
49922 Homestead Road
Oxbow, OR 97840
541-785-3373
www.hebb.us
$$ ☕
Near the Oxbow Dam Campground and post office.

Hell's Canyon RV Park, Cabins
Hwy 86
PO Box 243
Oxbow, OR 97840
541-785-3393, 800-453-3393
$
2 miles up road from Oxbow Dam Campground.

Hillside B&B
53875 Parker Road, Hwy 86
Oxbow, OR 97840
541-785-3389, 541-785-3335
$ ☕

CAMPING

Copperfield Park & Campground
Oxbow Dam
Oxbow, OR 97840
Park Information: 541-540-7209
Excellent riverfront campground.

In Route:
Woodhead Park & Campground
Brownlee Reservoir
541-540-7209
44.5 miles from Council.
Run by Idaho Power.

FOOD & DINING

Thompson's Hell Canyon Inn
53945 Hwy 86
Halfway, OR 97834
541-785-3383
Cocktails 7 days a week.

Hell's Canyon Store
53963 Hwy 86
Halfway, OR 97834
541-785-3330
Good for supplies.

Scotty's Hell's Canyon Outdoor Supplies
53969 Hwy 86
Halfway, OR 97840
541-785-3367

SPECIAL INTEREST

Hell's Canyon
More than 8,000 feet deep on the Snake River, Hell's Canyon is the deepest river gorge in North America. It is 22 miles long and spans the border between Idaho and Oregon.

RESOURCES

Hell's Canyon Recreation Report
Idaho Power
800-422-3143, 541-523-6391

Hell's Canyon Recreation Area
541-523-6391, 800-523-1235

Hell's Canyon Adventurers
541-785-3352
www.hellscanyonadventures.com

A road winds alongside the Snake River through Hell's Canyon.
Photo by Through The Lens Photography; IstockPhoto.

OREGON
9 Days - 482 Miles

From Idaho, you'll follow Adventure Cycling's route through Oregon to our recommended end-point on the coast at Florence. From there you can go up the coastal highway to Astoria, the end of the Lewis and Clark Trail (another AC destination not covered in this book) or catch the bus to Portland. No matter which way you go, peddling through Oregon shows you some of the best this pioneering state has to offer. Oregon is especially bicycle-friendly and so are its people.

OREGON FACTS & RESOURCES

Fast Facts
Population: 3.2 million
Capital: Salem
Nickname: The Beaver State
Flower: Oregon Grape
Bird: Western Meadowlark
Tree: Douglas Fir

Dates in History
1579 Sir Francis Drake discovers Oregon
1805 Lewis & Clark arrive in Washington
1843 Great Migration along the Oregon Trail begins
1859 Oregon becomes 33rd State

Oregon Tourism Commission
250 Church St SE, Ste 100
Salem, OR 97310
800-547-7842, 503-967-1560
www.traveloregon.com

Lewis & Clark Bicentennial in Oregon
503-390-2886
www.lcbo.net

Oregon State Parks
800-551-6949, 503-986-0707
www.oregonstateparks.org

Oregon Tourism Commission
250 Church St SE, Ste 100
Salem, OR 97310
800-547-7842, 503-986-0000
www.traveloregon.com

DAY 70 OXBOW (HELL'S CANYON) TO BAKER CITY, OR
Pop: 9,100   Mileage: 70.5
Est. Elevation: 4,200
AC Map: 3:24, 23, 22

Baker City — home to over 100 restored historic buildings, dating from the mid-1870s — is a good layover town because it's basically a week to the coast from here. Also, this is a tough day with 4,200 feet of climbing. You'll peddle through miles of Pine forests as you climb up Pine Creek with super views of the Wallowas, made famous as the legendary summer camp of the Nez Perce. At 17 miles you reach the town of Halfway with its entrance sign proclaiming "Half. com – America's first dot com city." After Halfway you make a 4.8-mile climb of switchbacks at 5 to 8 percent grade to a pass at 3,653 feet and then drop down into farm country and Richland and back to the Brownlee Reservoir. At 64 miles you reach the National Historic Oregon Trail Interpretive Center (not to be missed), and at 65.5 miles you'll cross Flagstaff Hill Pass at 3,684 feet and finally head down to Baker City.

PLACES TO STAY

Super 8 Motel
250 Campbell Street
Baker City, OR 97814
541-523-8282, 888-536-0729
$ 🛏🏊🖥

Always Welcome Inn
175 Campbell Street
Baker City, OR 97814
800-307-5206, 541-523-3431
$$ 🛏

Geiser Grand Hotel
1996 Main Street
Baker City, OR 97814
541-523-1889, 888-7374
$$$ 🍴
Completely restored 1889 hotel in historic district.

CAMPING

Oregon Trails West RV Park
42534 N Cedar Rd
Baker City, OR 97814
888-523-3236, 541-523-3236
All services.

**Mountain View Holiday
Trav-L Park**
2845 Hughes lane
541-523-4824
Great tent spot. 1.5 miles to
downtown on a paved path.

FOOD & DINING

Many choices but two favorites in
historic district:

Baker City Cafe
1840 Main St
Baker City, OR 97814
541-523-6099
Best clam chowder and
homemade pizza.

Barley Brown's Brew Pub
2190 Main St
Baker City, OR 97814
541-523-4266
Great food and beer.

SPECIAL INTEREST

**National Historic Oregon Trail
Interpretive Center**
22267 Hwy 86
Baker City, OR 97814
541-523-1843
$10 million center run by the
Bureau of Land Management
commemorating the trail. Half a
million immigrants took the Oregon
Trail from 1842 to 1869. One out
of 10 died in route. 7 miles before
Baker City on Hwy 86.
www.blm.gov/or/oregontrail

RESOURCES

Oregon Tourism Commission
800-547-7842
www.traveloregon.com

Baker County Visitors Center
490 Campbell
Baker City, OR 97814
800-523-1235, 541-523-5855
www.visitbakercity.com
Tourism officials call Baker City
"kind of the jackpot of history."

Dick's Bikes & Repair
2815 E Street
Baker City, OR 97814
541-523-7632

Today you'll climb 3,800 feet over three passes with high vistas of Eastern Oregon: Sumpter, 5,082 feet; Tipton, 5,124 feet; Dixie, 5,277 feet. You start the day on the Elkhorn Scenic Drive and at about 14 miles enter the Wallowa Whitman National Forest, where you begin your first climb through the pine forests. The town of Sumpter at about 28 miles is a good stop for food and water. At 45 miles you reach the summit at Tipton Station. Watch for occasional logging trucks. At 53 miles from Baker City is a junction with US 26 and the Austin House Restaurant and Grocery. Pick up supplies here if you're staying at Dixie Campground or Sags Motel. From the Dixie Summit it's downhill all the way to Prairie City, "Gateway to the Strawberry Mountain Wilderness," an old mining town with lots of small-town character all along Front Street.

PLACES TO STAY

Sag's Motel
69117 Hwy 26
Prairie City, OR 97869
541-820-4515
$
Closest motel option to Dixie Pass campground.

Strawberry Mountain Inn B&B
Hwy 26
Prairie City, OR 97869
800-545-6913, 541-820-4522
www.strawberrymountaininn.com
$$$$ ⫐
2.4 miles downhill from Sag's Motel.

CAMPING

Depot County Park
Main and Bridge Street
Prairie City, OR 97869
541-820-3605
Bathroom and showers. Next to the Museum.

Dixie Creek Campground
Hwy 26 at the Dixie Summit
Prairie City Ranger District
541-820-3800
Good water, no showers, no
reservations. Approx. 10 miles
from Prairie City.

Prairie City Visitor's Information
124 NW Front St
Prairie City, OR 97869
541-820-3739

FOOD & DINING

Food In Route:
McEwen Country Store
Hwy 7 outside Sumpter.

Chuck's Little Diner
142 Front Street
Prairie City, OR 97869
541-820-4353
Homemade treats.

SPECIAL INTEREST

DeWitt Depot Museum
Main and Bridge Streets next to
campground.
541-820-3598
Sumpter Valley Narrow Gauge
Railroad

This is an easy day of carefree bicycling, mostly downhill through juniper-covered hillsides and deep river canyons. You'll ride through the John Day River Valley to arrive in another small town with an original antique store and a one-room city hall at its entrance. Fans of Adventure Cycling cyclists, Dayville has hung a banner over main street: "Welcome TransAm Cyclists."

PLACES TO STAY

Fish House Inn B&B & RV
110 Franklin, Hwy 26
Dayville, Oregon 97825
888-286-FISH, 541-987-2124
$$ ☕

CAMPING

Fish House Inn B&B & RV
110 Franklin, Hwy 26
Dayville, Oregon 97825
888-286-FISH, 541-987-2124
$$ ☕

Dayville Presbyterian Church Hostel
PO Box 4
Dayville, OR 97825
541-987-2521
Has showers.

FOOD & DINING

Dayville Cafe
212 W Franklin Ave
Dayville, OR 97825
541-987-2122

SPECIAL INTEREST

Grant County Historic Museum
101 Canyon City East Rd
Canyon City, OR 97820
541-575-0362
Near John Day along the route, 13 miles from Prairie City. Open 7 days a week, various hours.

**Grant County Chamber of
Commerce**
301 W Main Street
John Day, OR 97845
541-575-0547

The "Open Road"
Photo Credit: Oregon Tourism Commission

DAY 73 DAYVILLE TO MITCHELL, OR
Pop: 230
Mileage: 39
Est. Elevation: 2,100
AC Map: 2:18, 17, 16

This short, 39-mile day can be combined with the following one to make 87.5 miles and 4,500 feet of climb. Either way, you'll start along the John Day River, enter a long gorge and once again climb into pine meadows. At 4.5 miles you enter the John Day Fossil Beds National Monument and at 5.5 miles, Picture Gorge. At 7 miles at the junction of OR 19 you can turn right two miles to the John Day Fossil Visitor Center. This convenient detour is highly recommended, especially if you're staying in nearby Mitchell, to experience a premier geologic site and learning adventure. At 32 miles you reach the Keyes Creek Summit, 4,369 feet and begin a 6 percent downhill into Mitchell. You'll zoom past an historical market for H.H. Wheeler, US Mail Carrier wounded at that spot. Mitchell is a rather funky old town that hasn't yet seen the restoration dollars of its neighbors but still has a certain appeal.

PLACES TO STAY

There's only one place:
The Oregon Hotel
104 Main St
Mitchell, OR 97750
541-462-3027
$$ ☕

CAMPING

Lion's Club Park
Main Street
Mitchell, OR 97750

Ochoco Divide Campground
State Forest Service Campground
541-416-6500
Ochoco Pass 16 miles past Mitchell.

FOOD & DINING

Wheeler County Trading Post
100 E Main Street
Mitchell, OR 97750
541-462-3117
Ken & Pat Bond. Groceries.

Little Pine Cafe
100 E Main St
Mitchell, OR 97750
541-462-3532
Local grits and gossip.

John Day Fossil Beds National Monument
Visitor Center
32651 Hwy 19
Kimberly, OR
541-987-2333
www.nps.gov/joda
North of Mitchell, open daily March through October. Contains one of the world's most complete fossilized records of natural history.

Mitchell Visitor Information
Wheeler Country General Store
City of Mitchell
Mitchell, OR 97750
541-462-3585
www.wheelercounty-oregon.com

Painted Hills near Mitchell, Oregon. Photo credit: Ray Atkenson

Note: The next three days are described as separate itineraries. If you're in a hurry to get to the coast, you can combine them into a two day alternative: Mitchell to Redmond, 71.5, and Redmond to McKenzie Bridge, 61.5.

This day is again full of pine stands and green meadows. At eight miles you begin your climb to Ochoco Pass at 4,720 feet and then descend through Ponderosa and open parklands. At 41 miles you reach Mill Creek Ochoco Reservoir, which has a nice campground only 7.5 miles east of Prineville. The town itself is a rockhound's paradise with the Chinese restaurant you've had a taste for the last 500 miles!!

PLACES TO STAY

Best Western Prineville Inn
1475 NE 3rd Street
Prineville, OR 97754
541-447-8080
$$ ⊓ ✕ ⛱

Stafford Inn
1773 NE 3rd Street
Prineville, OR 97754
541-447-7100
$$ ⊓ ⛱ ▣
www.staffordinn.com

Econo Lodge
123 NE 3rd St
Prineville, OR 97754
541-447-6231
$$ ✕

Rustlers Inn
960 NW 3rd Street
Prineville, OR 97754
541-447-4185
www.rustlersinn.com

CAMPING

Mill Creek Ochoco Reservoir Campground
541-416-6500
7.5 miles east of Prineville.

Crook County RV Park
1040 S Main St
Prineville, OR 97754
541-447-2599
Next to fairgrounds.

FOOD & DINING

Panda Restaurant
555 N Main Street
Prineville, OR 97754
541-447-8288
Great Chinese.

SPECIAL INTEREST

Bowman Museum
246 N Main St
Prineville, OR 97754
541-447-3715
National Register of Historic Places.

RESOURCES

Prineville Crook County Chamber of Commerce
785 NW 3rd St
Prineville, OR 97754
541-447-6304, 541-447-5816
Annual Rockhound Pow-Wow.

PLACES TO STAY

REDMOND, Pop: 7,200

Best Western Rama Inn
2630 SW 17th Place
Redmond, OR 97756
541-548-8080
$$ ⊃ ✕ ≋
Rama in Hindu means wealth and good fortune.

Redmond Super 8
3629 21st Place SW
Redmond, OR 97756
541-548-8881
$ ✕

Redmond Chamber of Commerce
446 SW 7th Street
Redmond, OR 97756
541-923-5191

CAMPING

Cascade Swim Center
465 SW Rimrock Way
Redmond, OR 97754
541-548-7275
Showers, pool, allows camping.
Call first.

DAY 75 PRINEVILLE TO SISTERS, OR
Pop: 1,080
Mileage: 41.5
Est. Elevation: <1,000
AC Map: 2:15, 14, 13

Editor's note: Map has a new routing through Redmond.

The first half of the day you ride through fragrant juniper trees and valley ranches along the aptly named Crooked River. At the top of a short ridge, 15 miles from Prineville, you'll enjoy a delightful view of the Oregon Cascades: Mt. Jefferson, Mt. Washington, Three Sisters and Mt. Bachelor and then head to bustling Redmond down the road. Sisters, 19 miles further down the road, is a quaint, boutique town with loads of lattes and flower baskets. The chamber urges you to: "Come and enjoy the Beauty of the Old West."

PLACES TO STAY

Best Western Ponderosa Lodge
505 Hwy 20. West end of town.
Sisters, OR 97759
541-549-1234
$$$ 🛏️🏊

Sisters Inn
605 Arrow Leaf Trail
Sisters, OR 97759
541-549-7829
$$$ 🛏️🍽️🏊

CAMPING

Sisters City Park
Off Junction US 20
Sisters, OR 97759
541-549-6022
One mile from town.

Circle 5 Campground
Off Junction US 20
Sisters, OR 97759
Name has recently changed. No number listed but it's still there according to locals. Two-tenths mile from city park.

FOOD & DINING

Bronco Billy's Ranch Grill & Saloon
190 E Cascade Ave
Sisters, OR 97759
541-549-RIBS- 7427
Great burgers and fries.

Angeline's Bakery & Cafe
121 W Main Street
Sisters, OR 97759
541-549-9122
Wonderful homemade muffins and scones.

SPECIAL INTEREST

Hotel Sisters
190 E Cascade Ave
Sisters, OR 97759
541-549-7427
Above Bronco Billy's Ranch Grill
and Saloon.
One of the last remaining historic
buildings, the Hotel Sisters has
been renovated and is now a
popular Western-style saloon and
restaurant.

RESOURCES

**Sisters Chamber of Commerce
Visitors Center**
291 E Main St
Sisters, OR 97757
541-549-0251
www.sisterscounty.com

Euro Sports Bike Shop
182 E Hood Avenue
Sisters, OR 97757
541-549-2471

*Broken Top Mountain, East of Sisters,
Oregon. Photo credit: Sharon Payne*

Note: Adventure Cycling provides an alternate, longer route over the lower Santiam Pass, which has more campgrounds and is open year-round. Our recommended route over McKenzie Pass is typically open July – October. Check with the Sisters Chamber for road conditions.

From Sisters you enter the Deschutes National Forest and follow the McKenzie National Scenic Highway 11 miles to the site of the Windy Point Eruption, which occurred 1,500 years ago. The area is covered with black lava fields from the eruption of Belknap Crater and Mt. Mazama. At 15.5 miles you reach the spectacular summit of McKenzie Pass at 5,325 feet. Take time to walk up the Dee Wright Observatory, where you can see all the way to Mt. Hood near Portland. Once over the pass you roll downhill past numerous campgrounds and lodges along the McKenzie River. Most significant during today's ride is the dramatic shift in forest plant zones as you ascend through the dry pine slopes of the eastern Cascades and descend into the wet western slopes with alpine fir, spruce, Pacific silver fir, Douglas fir, cedar and hemlock, all in one day.

PLACES TO STAY

Horse Creek Lodge
56228 National Forest Development Rd
Blue River, OR 97413
541-822-3243
Email: *reservations@horse-creek.com*
They offer shuttle service for cyclists.
$$$ $100-140

Cedarwood Lodge
56535 McKenzie Hwy
McKenzie Bridge, OR 97413
541-822-3351
www.cedarwoodlodge.com
$$$

CAMPING

**McKenzie Bridge Campground
National Forest**
McKenzie Bridge, OR 97413
877-444-6777, 541-225-6300

Patio RV Park
55636 McKenzie River Drive
Blue River, OR 97423
541-822-3596
Expensive camping, but only $2
shower per person.

FOOD & DINING

McKenzie Espresso & Deli
56393 McKenzie Highway
McKenzie Bridge, OR 97413
541-822-6006
Open Daily 8:30-2 pm.

Takoda's Restaurant
91806 Mill Creek Rd
Blue River, OR 97413
541-822-1153
2 miles west of McKenzie Bridge
Campground.
Good dining.

McKenzie Bridge General Store
56245 Delta Dr
McKenzie Bridge, OR 97413
541-822-3221
Est. 1900.

SPECIAL INTEREST

Dee Wright Observatory
McKenzie Summit in
Willamette National Forest.
Site of one of the most recent
volcanic lava flows in the US.
Lava River Interpretive Trail and
Observatory open July – October.

RESOURCES

**McKenzie River
Chamber of Commerce**
44643 McKenzie Hwy
Walterville, OR 97489
800-318-8819, 541-896-3330
Chamber is located along the
route in an old house. Free
hazelnut samples.

Today's ride is mostly a long, slow downhill along one of the most famous rivers in the Northwest, the McKenzie. From salmon and steelhead fishing in the upper foothills to the fertile lower valley, the route meanders through some of Oregon's most famous filbert (also known as hazelnut) farms. At 24 miles just beyond Vida is the Goodpasture Covered Bridge, built in 1938, one of five covered wooden bridges in this area. Congestion increases as you near Eugene. Follow the Adventure Cycling Eugene Spur route across the McKenzie and Willamette Rivers into the heart of Eugene near the University of Oregon campus. Eugene is a bicyclists' town, home of both Burley and Co-Motion Cycles.

PLACES TO STAY

ON ROUTE
The Campbell House
Inn & Restaurant
252 Pearl Street
Eugene, OR 97401
800-264-2519, 541-343-1119
www.campbellhouse.com
$$$

Timbers Motel
1015 Pearl Street
Eugene, OR 97401
800-643-4167, 541-343-3345
www.timbersmotel.net
$ 🏳

DOWNTOWN
Eugene Whiteaker
International Hostels
970 W 3rd Ave
Eugene, OR 97402
541-343-3335

Downtown Inn
361 W 7th Street
Eugene, OR 97401
800-648-4366
Convenient, accomodating, large rooms, clean, wifi access.
$$

CAMPING

Eugene Kamping World & RV Park
90932 S Stuart Street
Coburg, OR 97408
541-343-4832
2-3 miles north of Eugene.

FOOD & DINING

Toshi's Ramen
1520 Pearl St
Eugene, OR 97401
541-683-7833
Good sampling of inexpensive Japanese food.

Diablo's Downtown Lounge
959 Pearl
Eugene, OR 97401
541-343-2346

SPECIAL INTEREST

University of Oregon
1585 E 13th Ave
Eugene, OR 97403
541-346-3027
uoma.uoregon.edu
Famed Asian art collection in Museum of Art.

Collins Cycle Shop
60 E 11th Ave
Eugene, OR 97401
541-342-4878

Burely Design Cooperative
4020 Stewart Road
Eugene, OR 97402
541-687-1644
www.burley.com

CoMotion Cycles
4765 Pacific Avenue
Eugene, OR 97402
541-342-4583, 866-282-6336
www.co-motion.com

RESOURCES

Eugene Area Chamber of Commerce
1401 Willamette Street
Eugene, OR 97401
541-484-1314
www.eugenechamber.com

Eugene Visitors Center
754 Olive St
800-547-5445, 541-484-5307
www.eugenecascadescoast.org

Note: Exit town by using the Eugene inset on AC TransAm Map 1. At six miles switch to the Florence-Eugene alternate on the same map.

You'll travel today through some of the old-style sawmill towns and hollows of the Coastal Range down to the picturesque Oregon Coast. The town of Noti will remind you of some of the hollows in Appalachia 10 states ago. After Noti you follow busy Hwy 126 all the way to Florence. Check out historic Old Town in Florence, perched right on the Siuslaw River with its 60 shops and eateries along Bay Street. Have a beer, pizza or steak. You deserve it. Congratulations. You made it across America!

PLACES TO STAY

Accommodations listed are in or near Old Town:

River House Motel
1202 Bay Street
Florence, OR 97439
541-997-3933, 877-997-3933
$$$ ✕

Villa West Motel
901 Hwy 101
Florence, OR 97439
541-997-3457
$ ☕

Lighthouse Inn
155 Hwy 101
Florence, OR 97439
866-997-3221
www.lighthouseinn-florence.com
$$

Money Saver Motel
170 Hwy 101
Florence, OR 97439
541-997-7131
$

Edwin K B&B
1155 Bay Street
Florence, OR 97439
541-997-8360, 800-8EDWINK
$$ ☕

CAMPING

Port of Siuslaw RV Park & Marina
Old Town Loop
80 Harbor Street
Florence, OR 97439
541-997-3040
All facilities.

FOOD & DINING

Bridgewater Seafood Restaurant
1297 Bay Street
Florence, OR 97439
541-997-9405
Super clam chowder.

Traveler's Cove
1362 Bay Street
Florence, OR 97439
541-997-6845
Dining on a cozy waterfront deck.

B.J.'s Ice Cream Parlor
2930 US 101
Florence, OR 97439
541-997-7286
Non-fat frozen yogurt.

SPECIAL INTEREST

Historic Old Town
www.oldtownflorence.com

Oregon Dunes National Recreation Area
855 US 101
Reedsport, OR 97467
Reedsport Chamber Office
Oregon Dunes Visitor Center
541-271-3611
30,000 acres with dunes reaching 400 feet high. Dune-buggy heaven.

RESOURCES

Florence Chamber of Commerce
290 Hwy 101
Florence, OR 97439
541-997-3128
www.florencechamber.com

Bicycles 101
1537 8th Street
Florence, OR 97439
541-997-5717

Hecta Head Lighthouse near Florence, Oregon. Photo credit: Dennis Frates

ALTERNATE:
A Northern Route to
Seattle, Washington

Seattle skyline and Space Needle photo credit: Seattle-King County Convention and Visitors Bureau

The Northern Alternate
8 Days - 462.5 Miles

After traveling nearly 4,000 miles, we figured why not end this trip in a major metropolitan city like Seattle? Once there, you can dine, drink, and dance to your heart's content or catch a plane, bus, train or ferry to anywhere you like. Plus, since it's our hometown, destination Seattle seemed just right to us. Unfortunately, although the new Adventure Cycling Lewis and Clark maps cover part of the route, none exist at press time to take you all the way to Seattle. Consequently, you'll need to pick up a Washington highways map as you enter the state. Included for your convenience are cue sheets for each day in Washington.

The Northern Route to Seattle begins with Day 66 from Lowell and heads to Lewiston, Idaho. You also may want to pick up an Idaho map just to spot your route. At Lewiston you'll cross the Snake River and enter Washington, your final state.

Washington is almost like two completely different states: the eastern, dry, agricultural side and the wet, western, very green side. Known for its high profile companies like Microsoft, Boeing and Starbucks Coffee, Seattle is the 18th largest market in the US. It is also home to the largest water-based transportation system in the country, Washington State Ferries.

Fast Facts
Population: 5.6 million
Capital: Olympia
Nickname: The Evergreen State
Flower: Rhododendron
Bird: Goldfinch
Tree: Western Hemlock

Dates in History
1579 Sir Francis Drake discovers Pacific Coast
1792 Capt. George Vancouver discovers Puget Sound
1805 Lewis & Clark arrive in Washington
1889 Washington 42nd state

WA Travel Development Division
General Administration Bldg.
Olympia, WA 98504
800-544-1800
www.stayinwashington.com
www.experiencewashington.com

Washington State DOT
Bicycling Info and Map
360-705-7258
www.wsdot.wa.gov/bike

DAY 66 LOWELL or LOOKING GLASS TO LEWISTON, ID   Pop: 28,100   Mileage: 85
Est. Elevation: 500
AC Map: 3:30, 31 (Off Route at Kooskia. Use Idaho map)

Today you happily head north. From Lowell or Looking Glass you'll continue west on Hwy 12. At 11 miles you'll come to the intersection with SR 13. The Adventure Cycling route through Oregon turns left here. To go to Seattle, you continue straight on US 12 towards Lewiston. At 14 miles is Dale's Grocery Store, open 24 hours. Now you're following the Clearwater River and Canyon, full of osprey, Canada geese, kingfishers and salmon. At 33 miles is the Gold Rush Ferry, used to ferry miners back and forth during the Clearwater Gold Rush in 1860. At 38 miles is the site where Lewis and Clark launched their canoes and began their final water passage to the Pacific. It's a long day; so take a break and enjoy a Becky's Burger in historic Orofino at 42 miles. You'll ride through the Nez Perce Indian Reservation on the way to Lewiston, where the Clearwater empties into the Snake River.

PLACES TO STAY

Comfort Inn
2128 8th Avenue
Lewiston, ID 83501
208-798-8090
$$$ 🏊

Red Lion Hotel
621 21st Street
Lewiston, ID 83501
208-799-1000, 800-RED-LION
www.lewiston.redlion.com
$$$ 🍴🏊🔲

Day's Inn
3120 North & South Hwy
Lewiston, ID 83501
208-743-8808
$

CAMPING

Aht' Wy Plaza RV Park
17818 Nez Pierce Rd
Lewiston, ID 83501
208-750-0231
🏊🔲 groceries, casino.

FOOD & DINING

Food In Route:
Wide range of restaurants
everywhere.

Zany Graze
2004 19th Ave
Lewiston, ID 83501
208-746-8131
Fifties food and fare.

SPECIAL INTEREST

Lewis & Clark in Idaho
www.lewisandclarkidaho.org
In 1805-06 Lewis & Clark crossed
Idaho on the trail now made
famous.

**Lewis and Clark Center for Arts
& History**
208-792-2243
www.lcsc.edu/museum

Spalding Mission Marker
At 74 miles. Rev. Henry Harman
Spalding built a mission and
brought the first printing press to
the Northwest.

RESOURCES

Lewiston Chamber of Commerce
989-786-2293
www.lewistonchamber.org

DAY 67 LEWISTON, ID TO DAYTON, WA
Pop: 2,500
Mileage: 69.5
Est. Elevation: 3,500
Map: L&C Trail 7:99, 100, 101

If your image of Washington state is all green, this day will change your mind as you peddle through the suede-colored, dry wheat fields of Eastern Washington. Today's route is straightforward; you just stay on US 12 all day. The first few miles once you cross the river are flat along the Snake River Gorge, an area populated by great blue herons. At 4.8 miles you'll see the spot where Lewis and Clark first entered what is now Washington State on October 10, 1805. At 11.1 miles you pass the Alpowai Interpretive Center, which provides excellent information about the geology of the area and Lewis and Clark's trip down the Snake River. At 11.3 miles you begin a 12-mile up-grade that climbs approxi-mately 2,000 feet to the Alpowai Summit at 2,785 feet. The last four miles are steep; so save some energy. At the Summit take a break and survey the extensive wheat fields. Pomeroy at about 33 miles is a good place to have a snack before you head down into the Pataha Valley. Your second major uphill of 1,200 feet is the Willow Grade

at 61 miles. At 65.5 you reach Willow Summit, then head down to Dayton. This tiny restored town boasts 63 historic homes and seven buildings listed on the National Register of Historic Places.

PLACES TO STAY

The Weinhard Hotel
235 E Main Street
Dayton, WA 99328
509-382-4032
www.weinhard.com
$$$ ⌂ ✕

Blue Mountain Motel
414 W Main Street
Dayton, WA 99328
509-382-3040

The Purple House B&B
415 E Clay Street
Dayton, WA 99328
509-382-3159
$ ⌂

CAMPING

Lewis & Clark Trail State Park
36149 US 12
Dayton, WA 99328
509-337-6457
5 miles SW of Dayton on US 12.

FOOD & DINING

Weinhard Cafe
235 E Main Street
Dayton, WA 99328
509-382-1681
www.weinhard.com
Gourmet cafe.

SPECIAL INTEREST

Columbia County Courthouse, 1887
341 E Main St
Dayton, WA 99328
509-382-2131
Dayton, WA 99328

Dayton Historical Depot, 1881
Oldest courthouse and train depot in Washington state.

RESOURCES

Dayton Chamber of Commerce
166 E Main
Dayton, WA 99328
800-882-6299, 509-382-4825
www.historicdayton.com

Dayton Columbia County, Washington, Courthouse, 1887

CUE: LEWISTON TO DAYTON

69.5 miles, 3,500 ft

0.0 Ride downhill on 21st Street to US 12.

0.1 L on US 12 towards Clarkston, Washington. Numerous twists and turns as US 12 weaves through Lewiston.

1.1 Lewiston Levee trail on R. Continue on US 12.

2.4 Cross Snake River Bridge into Washington. Use caution. Consider the sidewalk if traffic is heavy.

3.6 City Center, Clarkston, Washington.

4.8 Information sign indicating location where Lewis and Clark began their journey down the Snake to the Pacific Ocean, October 10, 1805.

11.1 Alpowai Interpretative Center on R.

11.3 Begin 12.3-mile climb into the Columbia Plateau.

12.7 Banner Ranch (since 1888.)

19.5 Grade steepens.

23.6 Alpowai Summit, elevation 2,785. Take a break and enjoy the endless wheat fields stretching to the horizon.

32.5 Pomeroy. All Services. Continue on US 12.

56 Cross Tucannon River.

60 Begin 2nd major climb of day, 4.5 miles up Willow Grade.

63.1 False summit.

64.6 Willow Summit.

69.5 Dayton. End of segment. Hotels are in downtown Dayton. Camping is 5 miles southwest of Dayton on US 12.

Note: At 9.7 miles, if you prefer to head to Portland, Oregon, continue on US 12. Use the Adventure Cycling Lewis and Clark Bike Trail Map, Section 7, which will take you 275 miles to Portland.

From Dayton you follow the Touchet River to Richland, one of the nation's nuclear centers, also called "Atomic City." It is also part of Washington's Tri-Cities: Richland, Kennewick and Pasco. At 9.4 miles you reach the small town of Waitsburg for your first coffee stop at the Waitsburg Farmer's Cafe. At 9.7 as US 12 veers left be sure to make the right turn on SR 124 towards Prescott. Prescott at 18.6 miles has a grocery store and at about 31 miles a one-mile gentle climb to Eureka Flats is the only real climb of the day. Later you pass Charbonneau Park, named for Sacajawea's husband, and Ice Harbor Dam, one of many dams on the Snake River in the vast hydroelectric network of the Pacific Northwest. After crossing the Snake River, use the cue sheet which more or less follows the bike trail along the Columbia River. In Richland, there are a number of hotel options within a mile of the Columbia River bridge.

PLACES TO STAY

Hampton Inn
486 Bradley Blvd
Richland, WA 99352
509-943-4400, 888-370-0981
$$$ ⊐ ✕ ▣

Red Lion Hotel - Richland
802 George Washington Way
Richland, WA 99352
509-946-7611, 1-800-REDLION
$$ ⊐ ✕ ▣

Motel 6
1751 Fowler St
Richland, WA 99352
509-783-1250, 800-4MOTEL6
$

CAMPING

Columbia Park
Kennewick, WA
509-585-4529

Desert Gold Motel & RV Park
611 Columbia Park Trail
Richland, WA 99352
509-627-1000

Columbia River Journeys
1229 Columbia Park Trail
Richland, WA 99352
509-734-9941

FOOD & DINING

Many groceries, fast food, latte stands and restaurants.

Las Margaritas
627 Jadwin Avenue
Richland, WA 99352
509-946-7755

Sundance Grill
450 Columbia Point Drive
Richland, WA 99352
509-942-7120
Deluxe deck-side dining and bar on the Columbia River.

Atomic Ale Brewpub & Eatery
1015 Lee Blvd
Richland, WA 99352
509-946-5465
Super-charged burgers & brews.

SPECIAL INTEREST

Columbia River Sports
710 George Washington Way # F
Richland, WA 99352
509-946-7368
Boat and bike rentals.

RESOURCES

Richland Chamber of Commerce
7130 W Grandridge Blvd, Suite C
Kennewick, WA 99336
509-736-0510

Tri-Cities Visitor & Convention Bureau
7130 W Grandridge Blvd, Suite B
Kennewick, WA 99336
509-735-8486
www.visittri-cities.com

Tri-Cities Winery Guide
Tri-Cities Winery Association
509-588-6716
Includes over 40 wineries in the area.

Tri-Cities Bicycle Club
PO Box 465
Richland, WA 99352
ww.tricitybicycleclub.org
Tri-Cities Bike Path. 22 miles of super riding.

Columbia River Exhibition of History, Science & Technology
95 Lee Blvd
Richland, WA 99352
509-943-9000
www.crehst.org

70 miles, <1,000 ft

0.0   Downtown Dayton. Continue west on US 12.

.2   Cross Touchet River.

5.3   Lewis and Clark Trail State Park.

5.8   Cross Touchet River again.

9.4   Waitsburg.

9.7   Turn R on SR 124 towards Prescott as US 12 veers L. Note: If you are travelling to Portland, Oregon you would veer L staying on US 12.

13.6   Cross Touchet River.

18.6   Prescott. Grocery store. Continue on SR 124.

20   Continue straight on SR 124 as SR 125 intersects.

31   Begin gentle 1-mile climb to Eureka Flats.

46.6   Charbonneau Park at R.

49.7   Ice Harbor Dam at R.

55   Turn R onto US 12 towards Pasco. Divided highway begins.

55.4   Cross Snake River on US 12.

55.9   Cross Tank Farm Road.

56.7   L onto "A Street" (sign also says Port of Pasco.)

58.6   Cross Oregon Avenue (SR 397). Continue on "A."

59.6   Cross S 10th Avenue. Continue on "A."

61   As "A" Street ends and becomes 28th Avenue S, make a sharp L onto an unmarked paved bike path along the bank of the Columbia River.

61.4   Cross under Columbia River Bridge (US 395) on bike path.

66.5   Bike through Chiawana Park, staying on the bike path.

67.3   As bike path ends, turn L onto Court Street (bike lane.)

68.5   Immediately after crossing under I-82, make a sharp R onto a bike path which switchbacks up to the I-82 bridge and then heads west towards Richland.

68.8   Cross Columbia River using bridge bike path on the north side of I-82.

69.1   Immediately after crossing river use bike path to switchback down to R.

69.3   At the end of bridge bike path make L onto Columbia Point Drive. Bike lane.

69.7   R on Bradley Blvd. Bike lane.

70.1   Richland. End of segment. Various hotels on Bradley Blvd and along George Washington Way (arterial which parallels Bradley Blvd.+)

DAY 69 RICHLAND TO PROSSER, WA
Pop: 5,000   Mileage: 33
Est. Elevation: <1000
Map: WA State Hwy Map

This is a short day with no significant elevation. The reason we left it short is so you have lots of time to visit the wineries near Prosser, the site of Washington's first wine industry. You leave the Atomic City of Richland and travel about 15 miles through its outskirts to Benton City on the Yakima River. If you're hungry for bear-shaped pancakes, stop at the Bear Hut Restaurant. From Benton City you follow the Old Inland Empire Highway, also known as the OIEH, along the lower Yakima River through old orchards and farms and sparkling new vineyards on your way to Prosser.

PLACES TO STAY

Prosser Motel
1206 Wine County Road
Prosser, WA 99350
509-786-2555
$$

Best Western Prosser Inn
259 Merlot Drive
Prosser, WA 99350
509-786-7977, 800-780-7234
$$ ⛺︎🏊

River's Edge B&B
12901 S 1538 PR SW
Prosser, WA 99350
509-786-3060

CAMPING

Wine Country RV Park & Camping
330 Merlot Drive
Prosser, WA 99350
509-785-5192

FOOD & DINING

Food In Route:
Shadow Mountain Grill
623 9th Street
Benton City, WA 99320
509-588-3142
Baby bear pancakes.

The Red Barn (The Barn)
490 Wine Country Road
Prosser, WA 99350
509-786-2121
Old fashioned steaks and bar.

SPECIAL INTEREST

Benton County Historical Museum
1000 Paterson Rd
Prosser, WA 99350
509-786-3842
Open Tuesday-Sunday

Chukar Cherry Company
320 Wine Country Road
Prosser, WA 99350
800-624-9544
Samples of region's chocolate-covered cherries.

Wine tasting near town.

Hogue Cellars
2800 Lee Rd
Yakima, WA 98948
800-565-9779

Hinzerling Winery
1520 Sheridan Ave
Prosser, WA 99350
509-786-2163

Kestrel Winery
2890 Lee Rd
Prosser, WA 99350
509-786-2675

Yakima Valley Wine Association
www.yakimavalleywine.com
800-258-7270

RESOURCES

Prosser Visitor Information Center
1230 Bennett Avenue
Prosser, WA 99350
800-408-1517, 509-786-3177
www.prosserchamber.org

33 miles, <1,000 ft

0.0 Find the paved Columbia River bike path at river's edge behind hotels. Ride L (north) on the bike path.

1.4 Haines Street begins to parallel bike path at L.

1.6 L as bike path intersects Leslie Groves Park access road. Immediate R on Haines.

1.7 Curve L onto Van Giesen Avenue as Haines itself continues R and dead ends.

1.9 Cross George Washington Blvd. Continue on Van Giesen.

3.4 Cross busy SR 240 (aka Bypass Highway). Continue on Van Giesen as it becomes SR 224.

4.9 Cross Yakima River bridge into West Richland. Continue on SR 224.

13.3 Stay on SR 224 as it veers R.

13.5 R onto SR 225 across Yakima River bridge into Benton City. Bike lane.

14.9 Downtown Benton City. Bear Hut Restaurant at L.+

15.6 L onto "Old Inland Empire Highway" (aka "OIE Hwy").

27.6 Veer L at stop sign as OIE Hwy. veers L towards Prosser. Rothrock Road joins OIE Hwy. R. McCorkle's Market at intersection.

31.1 L at stop sign as Hinzerling Road joins OIE Hwy. N Prosser Market at junction.

31.5 Cross I-82 on overpass. Continue straight on Hinzerling Road as OIE Hwy turns R.

32.1 Cross Yakima River bridge into Prosser. Hinzerling Road becomes Grant Avenue.

32.6 Prosser. Intersection of Grant and Wine Country Road. End of segment. Prosser Motel is at intersection. L on 6th 0.3 miles to Visitors' Information and City Center. R on Wine Country Road to various accommodations and Wine Country RV Park.

Note: If you decide not to taste the spectacular wines in Prosser, this day can be combined with the previous one –Richland to Prosser – for an 84-mile fast-pass through the whole length of the Yakima Valley.

Leaving Prosser, the OIEH changes its name to the "Wine Country Road," also known as US 12, and you follow it or several optional bike paths which parallel it all the way to Sunnyside, "Home of astronaut Bonnie Dunbar." On your way you'll see Mt. Adams, one of the most beautiful snow-capped mountains of the Cascades, looming in the distance. Much of the bike path was built with funds from the Intermodal Surface Transportation Act, otherwise known as "Ice-Tea." It's positively flat all day as you head to Yakima, the "Fruit Basket of America." Grapes, and apple, peach, pear, apricot and plum orchards line the route. At 14 miles on the outskirts of Sunnyside the bike path ends at a Park 'N Ride, and Highway 12 changes its name once again, to the Yakima Valley Highway. As you depart, Mt. Adams looms closer (at 11 o'clock) and Mt. Rainier is just beginning to show its massive dome (at 2 to 3 o'clock). At 27 miles be sure to stop by the Tea Pot Dome Gas Station. Another great stop is in Zillah at about 28 miles for reputedly the most authentic Mexican food in the Northwest, served at El Ranchito and Tortilla Factory. After crossing under I-82 at 42 miles, the Yakima Valley Highway ends but the Sageland Winery is visible and immediately in front of you. This is the last chance for a winery visit in the Yakima Wine Country. You'll end the day at the outskirts of town near the new Yakima River Greenway.

PLACES TO STAY

On the Yakima River Greenway:
Oxford Inns
1603 E Yakima Avenue
Yakima, WA 98901
509-457-4444
$$$ ⛺🏊🔲

Oxford Suites
1701 E Yakima Ave
Yakima, WA 98901
509-457-9000
$$$ 🖤🏊◻

Birchfield Manor Country Inn
2018 Birchfield Road
Yakima, WA 98901
509-452-1960
$$$$ 🖤🏊
Big Splurge. Gourmet dinners.

CAMPING

KOA Campground
32 Thorp Hwy S
Yakima, WA 98901
509-925-9319

Sportsman State Park
904 University Parkway
Yakima, WA 98901
509-575-2774
1.5 miles from Birchfield Manor
on US 24.

FOOD & DINING

Many groceries, fast food and
restaurants.

Miner's Drive-In
2415 S First Street
Yakima, WA 98901
509-457-8194
Family-owned and-operated since
1948. Voted best burgers and fries
in the Valley.

SPECIAL INTEREST

Yakima Greenway
Greenway Foundation:
111 S 18th St
Yakima, WA 98901
509-453-8280
10-mile paved bike/walking path
from Selah Gap to Union Gap.
Greenway starts at Sherman
Memorial Park in Yakima.

Washington's Fruit Place & Gifts
1209 Pecks Canyon Rd
Yakima, WA 98901
509-966-1275
www.treeripend.com
Open Monday – Saturday. Free
samples and interpretive center.

Food In Route:
Dairygold Dairy Fair
400 Alexander Road
Sunnyside, WA 98944
509-837-8000
Cheese samples, cafe and self-
guided tour.

Sagelands Vineyard
71 Gangle Road
Wapato, WA
509-877-2112
Wine-tasting and snacks. Just
outside Yakima on route.

Teapot Dome Service Station
117 1st Ave
Zillah, WA 98953
509-829-5151
Shaped as a teapot, it is believed
to be the oldest operating gas
station in the US.

El Ranchito Restaurant Panaderia
1319 E 1st Avenue
Zillah, WA 98953
509-865-7709
.6 miles off route.

Yakima Valley Visitor's Bureau
& Convention Center
10 N 8th Street
Yakima, WA 98901
509-575-3010

Birchfield Country Manor, Yakima, Washington

51 miles, 1,000 ft.

0.0   Intersection of Grant and Wine Country Road (US 12). Take Wine Country Road over bridge towards Grandview.

.1   Cross Yakima River.

.2   Begin separated bike path at L. Follow bike path to Grandview and Sunnyside.

7.0   Enter Grandview. Exit bike path. Use wide shoulder through downtown Grandview.

8.4   Park and Ride lot at L. Begin riding on separated bike path again as it exits lot.

12.6 Enter Sunnyside.

14.2 Exit bike path at Park and Ride. Continue through Sunnyside on Yakima Valley Highway (US 12).

23.2 Cross Van Belle Rd (SR 223). Continue on Yakima Valley Highway.

27.6 Cross I-82 via underpass.+

29   Cross I-82 again via overpass. Zillah (El Ranchito Restaurant) is .6 miles off route to L on South 1st Avenue.

41.8 Continue on Yakima Valley Highway. Cross under I-82. Yakima River on L.

43.2 Cross under I-82. Yakima Valley Highway ends. L on Thorp.

43.3 Sagelands Winery entrance at R. Continue on Thorp.

44.9 Yakima River at L.

47.1 L on Birchfield Road (paved).

49.2 "Birchfield Manor" at L just before intersection with US 24.

49.3 L on US 24.

50.8 Sportsman Park on Yakima River. Camping. End of segment. Accommodations at Birchfield Manor or 2 miles ahead on Yakima River Greenway (Oxford Inn, Oxford Suites, see next segment).

Today you'll pass through two spectacular canyons. The first, Scenic Yakima River Canyon, comprises a 30 mile ribbon of endlessly curving, tightly twisting asphalt clinging to the flanks of a deep desert canyon as it leaves the Yakima River Valley. The second canyon is the Ellensburg Canyon, an old route now bypassed by the bigger I-90 highway, which fortunately you don't have to deal with, yet. As you depart Yakima you follow the Yakima Greenway path to the fruit distribution mecca of Selah. After Selah you travel the Yakima Scenic Canyon to the quaint college town of Ellensburg. Along the way you see much evidence of rugged geology carved by the Yakima River as it separates Eastern and Western Washington. From Ellensburg you follow lightly traveled US 10 to the Cascade-foothills town of Cle Elum, once a pine forestry center. Near here is the hamlet of Roslyn, where its admirers all know the TV show *Northern Exposure* was filmed.

PLACES TO STAY

Timber Lodge Inn
301 W First Street
Cle Elum, WA 98922
509-674-5966
$$ ▱ ▣

Stewart Lodge
805 W First Street
Cle Elum, WA 98922
509-674-4548, 877-233-5358
$$ ▱ ⟆ ▣

CAMPING

Whispering Pines RV Center
100 Whispering Pines Dr
Cle Elum, WA 98922
509-674-7278

FOOD & DINING

Various grocery and restaurants along First Street in Cle Elum.
Food In Route:
D&M Coffee Company
215 W 3rd Ave
Ellensburg, WA 98926
509-925-5313
Barista Extraordinaire.

The Cottage Cafe
911 E First Street
Cle Elum, WA 98922
509-674-2922
Open 24 hours.

El Caporal Mexican Restaurant
105 W First Street
Cle Elum, WA 98922
509-674-4284
Open 7 days a week, lunch and
dinner.

Cle Elum Chamber of Commerce
609 N Main St
Ellensburg, WA 98926
509-925-2002
www.kittitascountychamber.org

The beautiful scenic Yakima River Canyon, Washington

68 miles, 1,500 ft

0.0 Sportsman Park. Ride west on US 24 over Yakima River bridge.

.5 Stoplight at arboretum. Turn R and make an immediate second R onto arboretum frontage road.

.6 L into parking lot for Sherman Memorial Park. Find start of Yakima River Greenway Bike Path at edge of parking lot. Follow path west along the Yakima River.

5.3 Pass under I-82 (two bridges) on bike path.

5.4 Sharp L following bike path up onto second bridge, towards Selah.

7.0 Bike path ends. Continue straight ahead on 1st St through Selah.

7.8 R on Naches (SR 823).

8.0 L on N. Wenas (SR 823).

9.2 Veer R on Harrison (continuing on SR 823) at "Y" intersection.

10.7 Cross Yakima River bridge.

11.1 L on SR 821 towards Ellensburg.

13.5 Enter Historic Yakima River Canyon on SR 821. Follow 821.

36 Leave Yakima River Canyon and continue on Canyon Street.

39.5 Cross under I-90. Continue on Canyon, becomes Main Street, through Ellensburg.

41.7 L on 8th, becomes Cascade Way.

43.3 R on Reecer Creek Road.

43.4 L on US 10/US 97 (aka Dry Creek Conn.) towards Wenatchee.

45.7 Continue on US 10 towards Cle Elum as US 97 departs towards Wenatchee.

52.5 Enter Ellensburg Canyon on US 10 and follow to Cle Elum

62.3 Junction with SR 970. US 10 ends. L on SR 970 into Cle Elum. 970 becomes 1st Street E.

68 Midtown Cle Elum. Intersection of 1st and Pennsylvania Avenue. Segment ends. Camping on Oakes Avenue (SR 903) 1 block beyond Pennsylvania. Various motels along 1st Street.

From Cle Elum you travel through the famous Washington Cascades by way of Snoqualmie Pass with its many ski resorts and green, green forests. For this section of the trip your only choice is I-90, a major east/west thoroughfare varying from four to eight lanes. Despite the assault on your ears, there is a wide shoulder all the way to North Bend. There are also several one-to two-mile frontage-road loops where you can get a little respite from interstate truck traffic if you wish. At 32 miles you'll reach the Snoqualmie Summit with multiple lodgings in the winter. In the summer it's a good place to grab a snack or take a break before heading downhill towards Metropolis. North Bend is a little tourist town (with a big outlet center) most well known as the filming location for the movie *Twin Peaks*.

PLACES TO STAY

Roaring River B&B
46715 SE 129th Street
North Bend, WA 98045
425-888-4834
www.theroaringriver.com
$$$ ☕

Sunset Motel
227 W North Bend Way
North Bend, WA 98045
425-888-0381
$$

North Bend Motel
322 E North Bend Way
North Bend, WA 98045
425-888-1121
$$

CAMPING

Nor'West RV Park & Campground
45810 SE North Bend Way
North Bend, WA 98045
425-888-9685
Take Exit 34 off I-90 approx. 3 miles before town.

Blue Sky RV Park
9002 302nd Avenue SE
Issaquah, WA 98027
425-222-7910

Highland KOA
5801 S 212th St
Kent, WA 98032
253-872-8652

Snoqualmie Pass Visitor Information Center
425-434-6111

North Bend Ranger Station
425-888-1421

Summit Biking & Hiking Center
425-434-7669

FOOD & DINING

Twede's Cafe
137 W North Bend Way
North Bend, WA 98027
425-831-5511
Famous Twin Peak's cherry pie.

George's Bakery & Deli
127 W North Bend Way
North Bend, WA 98027
425-888-0632
The place to pick up a pastry.

Scott's Dairy Freeze Ice Cream
234 E North Bend Way
North Bend, WA 98027
425-888-2301
An institution for fast food in North Bend.

RESOURCES

Upper Snoqualmie Valley Chamber of Commerce
38767 SE River St
Snoqualmie, WA 98065
425-888-6362
www.snovalley.org

SPECIAL INTEREST

Snoqualmie Pass
First traveled in 1915, this pass connects rural Eastern Washington to Western Washington. Eateries and motels are located at the pass.

56 miles, 3,000 ft

0.0 Cle Elum. Continue west on 1st Street uphill towards Seattle and I-90 West.

.9 On ramp to I-90 West. Commence riding on highway shoulder.

3.2 Cross Cle Elum River. Continue on I-90 shoulder.

12.6 Take Exit #71 to Easton.

12.7 L over freeway towards Easton for a brief respite from I-90.

13.1 R on Railroad Street through Easton. Grocery at corner.

14.9 Take I-90 West on-ramp towards Seattle. Resume riding on highway shoulder.

24.7 Lake Keechelus on L.

27.3 I-90 West enters snow tunnel. Turn on flashers in tunnel.

32.2 Take Exit #53 to Snoqualmie Summit. L under freeway.

32.5 R to Summit West and Snoqualmie Pass Recreation Area.

33 Snoqualmie Summit. Traveler's Rest and various restaurants.

33.3 Return to I-90 West, now downhill towards Seattle.

53 Take Exit #32 to North Bend. Continue R on 436th Avenue SE.

53.8 L on SE North Bend Way towards downtown North Bend.

55.5 Middle of North Bend. Junction of SE North Bend Way and Bendigo Blvd (SR 202). End of segment. Various motels along SE North Bend Way. Camping is 3 miles BEFORE town at Exit 34.

The last day from North Bend to Seattle takes you through the remaining suburbs and into the major metropolis of downtown Seattle. Even though today's route is mainly downhill and short, you'll want the extra time to adjust and to navigate in the big city. If you're in a big hurry to get into Seattle, it's possible to combine this with the previous one to make 86 miles total. (We did it.) Bicycling on I-90 between Issaquah and Seattle is frowned upon. At 25 miles from North Bend, take the Sunset Exit off I-90 into the town of Issaquah and continue toward Seattle, using side roads and bike routes. Your first glimpse of Seattle comes as you follow a separated bike path alongside the Lake Washington Floating Bridge into the city. Once over the bridge, you have two good choices: Head through the bike pedestrian tunnel and go directly into the heart of downtown picturesquely located on the shores of Puget Sound. Or cycle north to the University of Washington and the "U" District.

Immediately after crossing the bridge, exit onto Lake Washington Blvd. and follow the signed bike path through the UW Arboretum to the University, a total distance of about seven miles from the bridge.

PLACES TO STAY

Mayflower Park Hotel
405 Olive Way
Seattle, WA 98101
206-623-8700
www.mayflowerpark.com
$$$ 🍵 ✗
Historic Hotel of America.

Holiday Inn Express – City Center
226 Aurora Avenue N
Seattle, WA
800-3152621, 206-441-7222
$$ 🍵

Best Western Pioneer Square Hotel
77 Yesler Way
Seattle, WA 98104
206-340-1234
$$$ 🍵

Hotel Deca
4507 Brooklyn Avenue
Seattle, WA 98105
206-634-2000
$$$ ⊔ ✕

University Inn
4140 Roosevelt Way NE
Seattle, WA 98105
206-632-5055
$$$ ⊔ ⌇ ▣

CAMPING

There are no campgrounds in the Seattle area proper; so your best bet is a hotel in the downtown or University District area. If you're camping, hop a ferry and go to Bainbridge Island to Fay Bainbridge State Park (7 miles from the Winslow ferry terminal). Pick up groceries in Winslow.

FOOD & DINING

Ivar's Acres of Clams
Pier 54
1001 Alaskan Way & Madison St
Seattle, WA
206-624-6852
Over 60 years old, the place on the waterfront for fish & chips.

House of Hong
409 8th Avenue S
Seattle, WA 98104
206-622-7997
Great Dim Sum lunch.

Sky City Restaurant
Atop Seattle Center Space Needle
400 Broad St
Seattle, WA 98109
206-905-2100
Take a spin around Seattle, 600 feet above ground.

SPECIAL INTEREST

It's totally impossible to list all the attractions in this fascinating coastal city and our hometown; so I recommend that you make a bee line for the Seattle-King County Convention and Visitor's Bureau and pick up information or check the web site. Here are just a few spots to add to your list:

Pike Place Market
International District
Seattle Center & Space Needle
Experience Music Project
Safeco and Seahawks Stadiums
Pioneer Square Historic District
Seattle Art Museum
Washington State Ferries
Seattle Waterfront

RESOURCES

Seattle-King County Convention & Visitors Bureau
701 Pike Street #800
Seattle, WA 98101
206-461-5800
www.visitseattle.org

University District Chamber of Commerce
4710 University Way NE, #114
Seattle, WA 98105
206-547-4417

University of Washington
206-543-2100
37,000 students and 700 acres located on the shores of Lake Washington.

Seattle Bicycling Map
One of the best places in the country to bicycle according to *Bicycling Magazine*, the city has a free bike map available at most bike shops and public libraries.
206-684-7583
www.seattlebicycle.com

R&E Cycles
5627 University Way NE
Seattle, WA 98105
206-527-4822

Cascade Bike Club
7400 Sand Point Way NE
Seattle, WA 98115
206-522-3222
www.cascade.org
Email: *info@cascade.org*

Bed & Breakfast Association of Seattle
PO Box 12031
Seattle, WA 98102
206-547-1020
www.lodginginseattle.com

Elliott Bay Bike Shop
2116 Western Ave
Seattle, WA 98121
206-441-8144

Gregg's Cycle
7007 Woodlawn NE
Seattle, WA 98115
206-523-1822

Lake Washington Floating Bridge

30 miles, <1,000 ft

0.0 Mid-North Bend. Junction of SE North Bend Way and Bendigo Blvd (SR 202). Continue west on North Bend Way (Business I-90).

1.9 Uphill. Continue on SE North Bend Way.

3.5 On ramp to I-90 West. Resume riding on highway shoulder.

12.6 Take Exit #18 (E Sunset Way) towards Issaquah. Continue on E Sunset Way.

13.5 Cross Front Street at stoplight. Continue on Sunset Way.

13.8 R on Newport Way.

14.8 L on Newport Way.

15.3 Cross Renton-Issaquah Road (SR 900). Continue on Newport Way.

16.4 Zoologic Park at L.

17.7 Cross W Lake Sammamish Way. Continue on SE Newport Way.

19.9 R on 153rd SE (bike sign). Speed bumps.

20.1 R on SE 39th.

20.2 L on 154th.

20.3 R on SE 38th (bike sign).

20.4 Continue on SE 38th through stop light on 150th. SE 38th becomes SE 36th.

21.9 Continue on SE 36th. Cross Richards Road using center left turn lane. Ride immediately onto sidewalk on SW corner of intersection and find bike path marked "I-90 Trail." Follow trail west alongside freeway.

22.2 Bike path intersects 118th Avenue SE. Cross street using crosswalk. Turn R on bike path on the south side of 118th SE.

22.3 L as bike path becomes a bike/pedestrian walkway through "Mercer Slough."

22.7 After climbing a short steep bridge, turn immediately L on bike path heading under freeway and towards "Enatai Beach Park" (and Seattle).

23   Stay on bike path as it turns R under freeway and switchbacks up to East Channel Bridge bike path towards Seattle.

23.6 After crossing bridge, follow Mercer Island bike route along I-90.

25.1 Continue as route briefly joins a sidewalk on north side of W Mercer Way.

25.6 Cross N Mercer Way at crosswalk. Continue R on bike route alongside freeway.

25.9 Bathrooms and water fountain in park. Follow bike route to L of bathrooms.

26.2 Cross W Mercer Way at crosswalk. Continue on bike path towards Seattle.

26.6 Cross Lake Washington using bike path alongside I-90 (Lacey Morrow) bridge.

28.2 After crossing Lake Washington, follow bike path as it switchbacks up to R. Stop at a viewpoint landing overlooking the bridge and lake. Decision point. If heading to downtown Seattle use Option A below. If heading to University of Washington, use Option B.

Option A: TO DOWNTOWN SEATTLE

28.3 From bridge viewpoint landing, enter the bike tunnel immediately behind you.

28.6 Exit tunnel and continue west on bike path. Cross MLK JR Way.

28.9 Cross 23rd Street. Continue on bike path curving to R.

29.3 As bike path ends, continue R (north) 2 blocks on busy Rainier Avenue.

29.6 Use L turn lane at stoplight to make L on Dearborn. Bike lane begins.

30   Continue on Dearborn under I-5.

30.4 Dearborn curves R and merges with Airport Way, then curves R again and merges with 4th Avenue. Continue in bike lane with flow of traffic.

30.6 4th and Jackson. End of segment. Continue on 4th to numerous downtown hotels. Turn L on Jackson 4 blocks to Seattle's waterfront and waterfront hotels.

CONGRATULATIONS, YOU MADE IT!

Option B: TO UNIVERSITY OF WASHINGTON

28.2 Do not enter bike tunnel. From bridge viewpoint turn R (north) and climb a short 1/2 block hill on Irving Street to intersection with Lake Washington Blvd S.

28.3 R on Lake Washington Blvd S.

28.9 Stop sign at 34th S. Pass through intersection and curve L following Lake Washington Blvd S. (Bike route sign).

29.3 Stop sign at Lakeside Avenue. L following Lake Washington Blvd.

29.7 Madrona Beach Park at R. Public bathrooms. Continue on Lake Wash Blvd.

29.9 Stop sign at Madrona Drive. Continue on Lake Washington Blvd.

30.6 Stop sign at 39th Avenue E. Continue straight on Lake Wash Blvd, winding up hill. Do not turn right on McGilvra Blvd E.

30.9 At top of hill turn L on E Harrison.

31.1 Cross 32nd Ave E. Continue on E. Harrison.

31.3 R at stop sign onto Martin Luther King Jr. Way. (Bike route sign).

31.4 Cross E Madison Street. Make quick R and L following MLK Jr. Way.

31.5 MLK Jr. Way becomes 28th Avenue E Continue on 28th Ave E.

31.9 28th Ave E becomes 26th Avenue E Continue on 26th Ave E.

32 L on E Galer Street.

32.1 R on 26th Avenue E.

32.2 Stop sign at Boyer Avenue E. Continue straight on 26th Avenue E. (Bike sign).

32.6 L on E Lynn Street.

32.7 R on 25th Ave E. (Bike route sign).

32.9 L on E Roanoke Street.

33 Stop sign. R on busy Montlake Place E.

33.1 Cross Lake Washington Blvd at stop light. Continue on Montlake Blvd. E.

33.3 Use sidewalk to cross Montlake Bridge over Lake Washington Ship Canal.

33.4 Intersection of Montlake Blvd and NE Pacific Street. End of segment. University of Washington campus visible across intersection. Various hotels, hostels, dormitories in campus area.

CONGRATULATIONS YOU MADE IT!

Your Feedback Please.

We hope you enjoyed using this book. If along the route you noticed any changes that would be helpful to share with other cyclists, please fill this out this form and mail it back. We'll try to include your suggestions in our next edition. Alternatively, you can e-mail us at: Whitedogpress@aol.com

1. Any corrections to the phone numbers or addresses, etc?

2. Any new food or motel stops along the way?

3. Any new or better campgrounds?

4. Any bike shops you'd like us to include?

Thank you very much,

Stephanie Ager Kirz
Publisher
White Dog Press, Ltd.
321 High School Road, Ste D3, PMB 393
Bainbridge Island, WA 98110
Whitedogpress@aol.com

CPSIA information can be obtained
at www.ICGtesting.com
Printed in the USA
FSOW03n0202311216
29035FS